THE BREATH OF LIFE

John Burroughs

1st WORLD
LIBRARY
Literary Society

The Breath of Life

John Burroughs

© 1st World Library, 2006
PO Box 2211
Fairfield, IA 52556
www.1stworldlibrary.com
First Edition

LCCN: 2006907722

Softcover ISBN: 1-4218-2433-7
Hardcover ISBN: 1-4218-2333-0
eBook ISBN: 1-4218-2533-3

Purchase *"The Breath of Life"*
as a traditional bound book at:
www.1stWorldLibrary.com/purchase.asp?ISBN=1-4218-2433-7

1st World Library is a literary, educational organization
dedicated to:

- Creating a free internet library of downloadable ebooks

  - Hosting writing competitions and offering book
    publishing scholarships.

1st World Library Literary Society

Giving Back to the World

"If you want to work on the core problem, it's early school literacy."

- James Barksdale, former CEO of Netscape

"No skill is more crucial to the future of a child, or to a democratic and prosperous society, than literacy."

- Los Angeles Times

Literacy... means far more than learning how to read and write... The aim is to transmit... knowledge and promote social participation."

- UNESCO

"Literacy is not a luxury, it is a right and a responsibility. If our world is to meet the challenges of the twenty-first century we must harness the energy and creativity of all our citizens."

- President Bill Clinton

"Parents should be encouraged to read to their children, and teachers should be equipped with all available techniques for teaching literacy, so the varying needs and capacities of individual kids can be taken into account."

- Hugh Mackay

PREFACE

As life nears its end with me, I find myself meditating more and more upon the mystery of its nature and origin, yet without the least hope that I can find out the ways of the Eternal in this or in any other world. In these studies I fancy I am about as far from mastering the mystery as the ant which I saw this morning industriously exploring a small section of the garden walk is from getting a clear idea of the geography of the North American Continent. But the ant was occupied and was apparently happy, and she must have learned something about a small fraction of that part of the earth's surface.

I have passed many pleasant summer days in my hay-barn study, or under the apple trees, exploring these questions, and though I have not solved them, I am satisfied with the clearer view I have given myself of the mystery that envelops them. I have set down in these pages all the thoughts that have come to me on this subject. I have not aimed so much at consistency as at clearness and definiteness of statement, letting my mind drift as upon a shoreless sea. Indeed, what are such questions, and all other ultimate questions, but shoreless seas whereon the chief reward of the navigator is the joy of the adventure?

Sir Thomas Browne said, over two hundred years ago, that in philosophy truth seemed double-faced, by which I fancy he meant that there was always more than one point of view of all great problems, often contradictory points of view, from which truth is revealed. In the following pages I am aware that two ideas, or principles, struggle in my mind for mastery. One is the idea of the super-mechanical and the super-chemical character of living things; the other is the idea of the supremacy and universality of what we call natural law. The first probably springs from my inborn idealism and literary habit of mind; the second from my love of nature and my scientific bent. It is hard for me to reduce the life impulse to a level with common material forces that shape and control the world of inert matter, and it is equally hard for me to reconcile my reason to the introduction of a new principle, or to see anything in natural processes that savors of the *ab-extra*. It is the working of these two different ideas in my mind that seems to give rise to the obvious contradictions that crop out here and there throughout this volume. An explanation of life phenomena that savors of the laboratory and chemism repels me, and an explanation that savors of the theological point of view is equally distasteful to me. I crave and seek a natural explanation of all phenomena upon this earth, but the word "natural" to me implies more than mere chemistry and physics. The birth of a baby, and the blooming of a flower, are natural events, but the laboratory methods forever fail to give us the key to the secret of either.

I am forced to conclude that my passion for nature and for all open-air life, though tinged and stimulated by science, is not a passion for pure science, but for literature and philosophy. My imagination and ingrained humanism are appealed to by the facts and methods of natural history. I find something akin to poetry and religion (using the latter word in its non-mythological sense, as indicating the sum of mystery and reverence we feel in the presence of the great facts of life and death) in the shows of day and night, and in my excursions to fields and woods. The love of nature is a different thing from the love of science, though the two may go together. The Wordsworthian sense in nature, of "something far more deeply interfused" than the principles of exact science, is probably the source of nearly if not quite all that this volume holds. To the rigid man of science this is frank mysticism; but without a sense of the unknown and unknowable, life is flat and barren. Without the emotion of the beautiful, the sublime, the mysterious, there is no art, no religion, no literature. How to get from the clod underfoot to the brain and consciousness of man without invoking something outside of, and superior to, natural laws, is the question. For my own part I content myself with the thought of some unknown and doubtless unknowable tendency or power in the elements themselves - a kind of universal mind pervading living matter and the reason of its living, through which the whole drama of evolution is brought about.

This is getting very near to the old teleological conception, as it is also near to that of Henri Bergson and Sir Oliver Lodge. Our minds easily slide into the groove of supernaturalism and spiritualism because they have long moved therein. We have the words and they mould our thoughts. But science is fast teaching us that the universe is complete in itself; that whatever takes place in matter is by virtue of the force of matter; that it does not defer to or borrow from some other universe; that there is deep beneath deep in it; that gross matter has its interior in the molecule, and the molecule has its interior in the atom, and the atom has its interior in the electron, and that the electron is matter in its fourth or non-material state - the point where it touches the super-material. The transformation of physical energy into vital, and of vital into mental, doubtless takes place in this invisible inner world of atoms and electrons. The electric constitution of matter is a deduction of physics. It seems in some degree to bridge over the chasm between what we call the material and the spiritual. If we are not within hailing distance of life and mind, we seem assuredly on the road thither. The mystery of the transformation of the ethereal, imponderable forces into the vital and the mental seems quite beyond the power of the mind to solve. The explanation of it in the bald terms of chemistry and physics can never satisfy a mind with a trace of idealism in it.

The greater number of the chapters of this volume are variations upon a single theme, - what Tyndall called "the mystery and the miracle of vitality," - and I can only hope that the variations are of sufficient interest to justify the inevitable repetitions which occur. I am no more inclined than Tyndall was to believe in miracles unless we name everything a miracle, while at the same time I am deeply impressed with the inadequacy of all known material forces to account for the phenomena of living things.

That word of evil repute, materialism, is no longer the black sheep in the flock that it was before the advent of modern transcendental physics. The spiritualized materialism of men like Huxley and Tyndall need not trouble us. It springs from the new conception of matter. It stands on the threshold of idealism or mysticism with the door ajar. After Tyndall had cast out the term "vital force," and reduced all visible phenomena of life to mechanical attraction and repulsion, after he had exhausted physics, and reached its very rim, a mighty mystery still hovered beyond him. He recognized that he had made no step toward its solution, and was forced to confess with the philosophers of all ages that

> "We are such stuff
> As dreams are made on, and our little life
> Is rounded with a sleep."

CONTENTS

I

THE BREATH OF LIFE

I

When for the third or fourth time during the spring or summer I take my hoe and go out and cut off the heads of the lusty burdocks that send out their broad leaves along the edge of my garden or lawn, I often ask myself, "What is this thing that is so hard to scotch here in the grass?" I decapitate it time after time and yet it forthwith gets itself another head. We call it burdock, but what is burdock, and why does it not change into yellow dock, or into a cabbage? What is it that is so constant and so irrepressible, and before the summer is ended will be lying in wait here with its ten thousand little hooks to attach itself to every skirt or bushy tail or furry or woolly coat that comes along, in order to get free transportation to other lawns and gardens, to green fields and pastures new?

It is some living thing; but what is a living thing, and how does it differ from a mechanical and non-living thing? If I smash or overturn the sundial with my hoe, or break the hoe itself, these things stay smashed and broken, but the burdock mends itself, renews itself, and, if I am not on my guard, will surreptitiously mature some of the burs before the season is passed.

Evidently a living thing is radically different from a mechanical thing; yet modern physical science tells me that the burdock is only another kind of machine, and manifests nothing but the activity of the mechanical and chemical principles that we see in operation all about us in dead matter; and that a little different mechanical arrangement of its ultimate atoms would turn it into a yellow dock or into a cabbage, into an oak or into a pine, into an ox or into a man.

I see that it is a machine in this respect, that it is set going by a force exterior to itself - the warmth of the sun acting upon it, and upon the moisture in the soil; but it is unmechanical in that it repairs itself and grows and reproduces itself, and after it has ceased running can never be made to run again. After I have reduced all its activities to mechanical and chemical principles, my mind seems to see something that chemistry and mechanics do not explain - something that avails itself of these forces, but is not of them. This may be only my anthropomorphic way of looking at things, but are not all our ways of looking at things anthropomorphic? How can they be any other? They cannot be deific since we are not gods. They may be scientific. But what is science but a kind of anthropomorphism? Kant wisely said, "It sounds at first singular, but is none the less certain, that the understanding does not derive its laws from nature, but prescribes them to nature." This is the anthropomorphism of science.

If I attribute the phenomenon of life to a vital force or principle, am I any more unscientific than I am when I give a local habitation and a name to any other causal force, as gravity, chemical affinity, cohesion, osmosis, electricity, and so forth? These terms stand for certain special activities in nature and are as much the inventions of our own minds as are any of the rest of our ideas.

We can help ourselves out, as Haeckel does, by calling the physical forces - such as the magnet that attracts the iron filings, the powder that explodes, the steam that drives the locomotive, and the like - "living inorganics," and looking upon them as acting by "living force as much as the sensitive mimosa does when it contracts its leaves at touch." But living force is what we are trying to differentiate from mechanical force, and what do we gain by confounding the two? We can only look upon a living body as a machine by forming new conceptions of a machine - a machine utterly unmechanical, which is a contradiction of terms.

A man may expend the same kind of force in thinking that he expends in chopping his wood, but that fact does not put the two kinds of activity on the same level. There is no question but that the food consumed is the source of the energy in both cases, but in the one the energy is muscular, and in the other it is nervous. When we speak of mental or spiritual force, we have as distinct a conception as when we speak of physical force. It requires physical force to produce the effect that we call mental force, though how the one can result in the other is past understanding. The law of the correlation and conservation of energy requires that what goes into the body as physical force must come out in some form of physical force - heat, light, electricity, and so forth.

Science cannot trace force into the mental realm and connect it with our states of consciousness. It loses track of it so completely that men like Tyndall and Huxley and Spencer pause before it as an inscrutable mystery, while John Fiske helps himself out with the conception of the soul as quite independent of the body, standing related to it as the musician is related to his instrument. This idea is the key to Fiske's proof of the immortality of the soul. Finding himself face to face with an insoluble mystery, he cuts the knot, or rather, clears the chasm, by this extra-scientific leap. Since the soul, as we know it, is inseparably bound up with physical conditions, it seems to me that a more rational explanation of the phenomenon of mentality is the conception that the physical force and substance that we use up in a mental effort or emotional experience gives rise, through some unknown kind of molecular activity, to something which is analogous to the electric current in a live wire, and which traverses the nerves and results in our changing states of consciousness. This is the mechanistic explanation of mind, consciousness, etc., but it is the only one, or kind of one, that lends itself to scientific interpretation. Life, spirit, consciousness, may be a mode of motion as distinct from all other modes of motion, such as heat, light, electricity, as these are distinct from each other.

When we speak of force of mind, force of character, we of course speak in parables, since the force here alluded to is an experience of our own minds entirely and would not suffice to move the finest dust-particle in the air.

There could be no vegetable or animal life without the sunbeam, yet when we have explained or accounted for the growth of a tree in terms of the chemistry and physics of the sunbeam, do we not have to figure to ourselves something in the tree that avails itself of this chemistry, that uses it and profits by it? After this mysterious something has ceased to operate, or play its part, the chemistry of the sunbeam is no longer effective, and the tree is dead.

Without the vibrations that we call light, there would have been no eye. But, as Bergson happily says, it is not light passively received that makes the eye; it is light meeting an indwelling need in the organism, which amounts to an active creative principle, that begets the eye. With fish in underground waters this need does not arise; hence they have no sight. Fins and wings and legs are developed to meet some end of the organism, but if the organism were not charged with an expansive or developing force or impulse, would those needs arise?

Why should the vertebrate series have risen through the fish, the reptile, the mammal, to man, unless the manward impulse was inherent in the first vertebrate; something that struggled, that pushed on and up from the more simple to the more complex forms? Why did not unicellular life always remain unicellular? Could not the environment have acted upon it endlessly without causing it to change toward higher and more complex forms, had there not been some indwelling aboriginal tendency toward these forms? How could natural selection, or any other process of selection, work upon species to modify them, if there were not something in species pushing out and on, seeking new ways, new forms, in fact some active principle that is modifiable?

Life has risen by stepping-stones of its dead self to higher things. Why has it risen? Why did it not keep on the same level, and go through the cycle of change, as the inorganic does, without attaining to higher forms? Because, it may be replied, it was life, and not mere matter and motion - something that lifts matter and motion to a new plane.

Under the influence of the life impulse, the old routine of matter - from compound to compound, from solid to fluid, from fluid to gaseous, from rock to soil, the cycle always ending where it began - is broken into, and cycles of a new order are instituted. From the stable equilibrium which dead matter is always seeking, the same matter in the vital circuit is always seeking the state of unstable equilibrium, or rather is forever passing between the two, and evolving the myriad forms of life in the passage. It is hard to think of the process as the work of the physical and chemical forces of inorganic nature, without supplementing them with a new and different force.

The forces of life are constructive forces, and they are operative in a world of destructive or disintegrating forces which oppose them and which they overcome. The physical and chemical forces of dead matter are at war with the forces of life, till life overcomes and uses them.

The mechanical forces go on repeating or dividing through the same cycles forever and ever, seeking a stable condition, but the vital force is inventive and creative and constantly breaks the repose that organic nature seeks to impose upon it.

External forces may modify a body, but they cannot develop it unless there is something in the body waiting to be developed, craving development, as it were. The warmth and moisture in the soil act alike upon the grains of sand and upon the seed-germs; the germ changes into something else, the sand does not. These agents liberate a force in the germ that is not in the grain of sand. The warmth of the brooding fowl does not spend itself upon mere passive, inert matter (unless there is a china egg in the nest), but upon matter straining upon its leash, and in a state of expectancy. We do not know how the activity of the molecules of the egg differs from the activity of the molecules of the pebble, under the influence of warmth, but we know there must be a difference between the interior movements of organized and unorganized matter.

Life lifts inert matter up into a thousand varied and beautiful forms and holds it there for a season, - holds it against gravity and chemical affinity, though you may say, if you please, not without their aid, - and then in due course lets go of it, or abandons it, and lets it fall back into the great sea of the inorganic. Its constant tendency is to fall back; indeed, in animal life it does fall back every moment; it rises on the one hand, serves its purpose of life, and falls back on the other. In going through the cycle of life the mineral elements experience some change that chemical analysis does not disclose - they are the more readily absorbed again by life. It is as if the elements had profited in some way under the tutelage of life. Their experience has been a unique and exceptional one. Only a small fraction of the sum total of the inert matter of the globe can have this experience. It must first go through the vegetable cycle before it can be taken up by the animal. The only things we can take directly from the inorganic world are water and air; and the function of water is largely a mechanical one, and the function of air a chemical one.

I think of the vital as flowing out of the physical, just as the psychical flows out of the vital, and just as the higher forms of animal life flow out of the lower. It is a far cry from man to the dumb brutes, and from the brutes to the vegetable world, and from the vegetable to inert matter; but the germ and start of each is in the series below it. The living came out of the not-living. If life is of physico-chemical origin, it is so by transformations and translations that physics cannot explain.

The butterfly comes out of the grub, man came out of the brute, but, as Darwin says, "not by his own efforts," any more than the child becomes the man by its own efforts.

The push of life, of the evolutionary process, is back of all and in all. We can account for it all by saying the Creative Energy is immanent in matter, and this gives the mind something to take hold of.

II

According to the latest scientific views held on the question by such men as Professor Loeb, the appearance of life on the globe was a purely accidental circumstance. The proper elements just happened to come together at the right time in the right proportions and under the right conditions, and life was the result. It was an accident in the thermal history of the globe. Professor Loeb has lately published a volume of essays and addresses called "The Mechanistic Conception of Life," enforcing and illustrating this view. He makes war on what he terms the metaphysical conception of a "life-principle" as the key to the problem, and urges the scientific conception of the adequacy of mechanico-chemical forces. In his view, we are only chemical mechanisms; and all our activities, mental and physical alike, are only automatic responses to the play of the blind, material forces of external nature. All forms of life, with all their wonderful adaptations, are only the chance happenings of the blind gropings and clashings of dead matter: "We eat, drink, and reproduce [and, of course, think and speculate and write books on the problems of life], not because mankind has reached an agreement that this is desirable, but because, machine-like, we are compelled to do so!"

He reaches the conclusion that all our inner subjective life is amenable to physico-chemical analysis, because many cases of simple animal instinct and will can be explained on this basis - the basis of animal tropism. Certain animals creep or fly to the light, others to the dark, because they cannot help it. This is tropism. He believes that the origin of life can be traced to the same physico-chemical activities, because, in his laboratory experiments, he has been able to dispense with the male principle, and to fertilize the eggs of certain low forms of marine life by chemical compounds alone. "The problem of the beginning and end of individual life is physico-chemically clear" - much clearer than the first beginnings of life. All individual life begins with the egg, but where did we get the egg? When chemical synthesis will give us this, the problem is solved. We can analyze the material elements of an organism, but we cannot synthesize them and produce the least spark of living matter. That all forms of life have a mechanical and chemical basis is beyond question, but when we apply our analysis to them, life evaporates, vanishes, the vital processes cease. But apply the same analysis to inert matter, and only the form is changed.

Professor Loeb's artificially fathered embryo and starfish and sea-urchins soon die. If his chemism could only give him the mother-principle also! But it will not. The mother-principle is at the very foundations of the organic world, and defies all attempts of chemical synthesis to reproduce it.

It would be presumptive in the extreme for me to question Professor Loeb's scientific conclusions; he is one of the most eminent of living experimental biologists. I would only dissent from some of his philosophical conclusions. I dissent from his statement that only the mechanistic conception of life can throw light on the source of ethics. Is there any room for the moral law in a world of mechanical determinism? There is no ethics in the physical order, and if humanity is entirely in the grip of that order, where do moral obligations come in? A gun, a steam-engine, knows no ethics, and to the extent that we are compelled to do things, are we in the same category. Freedom of choice alone gives any validity to ethical consideration. I dissent from the idea to which he apparently holds, that biology is only applied physics and chemistry. Is not geology also applied physics and chemistry? Is it any more or any less? Yet what a world of difference between the two - between a rock and a tree, between a man and the soil he cultivates. Grant that the physical and the chemical forces are the same in both, yet they work to such different ends in each. In one case they are tending always to a deadlock, to the slumber of a static equilibrium; in the other they are ceaselessly striving to reach a state of dynamic activity - to build up a body that hangs forever between a state of integration and disintegration. What is it that determines this new mode and end of their activities?

In all his biological experimentation, Professor Loeb starts with living matter and, finding its processes capable of physico-chemical analysis, he hastens to the conclusion that its genesis is to be accounted for by the action and interaction of these principles alone.

In the inorganic world, everything is in its place through the operation of blind physical forces; because the place of a dead thing, its relation to the whole, is a matter of indifference. The rocks, the hills, the streams are in their place, but any other place would do as well. But in the organic world we strike another order - an order where the relation and subordination of parts is everything, and to speak of human existence as a "matter of chance" in the sense, let us say, that the forms and positions of inanimate bodies are matters of chance, is to confuse terms.

Organic evolution upon the earth shows steady and regular progression; as much so as the growth and development of a tree. If the evolutionary impulse fails on one line, it picks itself up and tries on another, it experiments endlessly like an inventor, but always improves on its last attempts. Chance would have kept things at a standstill; the principle of chance, give it time enough, must end where it began. Chance is a man lost in the woods; he never arrives; he wanders aimlessly. If evolution pursued a course equally fortuitous, would it not still be wandering in the wilderness of the chaotic nebulae?

III

A vastly different and much more stimulating view of life is given by Henri Bergson in his "Creative Evolution." Though based upon biological science, it is a philosophical rather than a scientific view, and appeals to our intuitional and imaginative nature more than to our constructive reason. M. Bergson interprets the phenomena of life in terms of spirit, rather than in terms of matter as does Professor Loeb. The word "creative" is the key-word to his view. Life is a creative impulse or current which arose in matter at a certain time and place, and flows through it from form to form, from generation to generation, augmenting in force as it advances. It is one with spirit, and is incessant creation; the whole organic world is filled, from bottom to top, with one tremendous effort. It was long ago felicitously stated by Whitman in his "Leaves of Grass," "Urge and urge, always the procreant urge of the world."

This conception of the nature and genesis of life is bound to be challenged by modern physical science, which, for the most part, sees in biology only a phase of physics; but the philosophic mind and the trained literary mind will find in "Creative Evolution" a treasure-house of inspiring ideas, and engaging forms of original artistic expression. As Mr. Balfour says, "M. Bergson's 'Evolution Creatrice' is not merely a philosophical treatise, it has all the charm and all the audacities of a work of art, and as such defies adequate reproduction."

It delivers us from the hard mechanical conception of determinism, or of a closed universe which, like a huge manufacturing plant, grinds out vegetables and animals, minds and spirits, as it grinds out rocks and soils, gases and fluids, and the inorganic compounds.

With M. Bergson, life is the flowing metamorphosis of the poets, - an unceasing becoming, - and evolution is a wave of creative energy overflowing through matter "upon which each visible organism rides during the short interval of time given it to live." In his view, matter is held in the iron grip of necessity, but life is freedom itself. "Before the evolution of life ... the portals of the future remain wide open. It is a creation that goes on forever in virtue of an initial movement. This movement constitutes the unity of the organized world - a prolific unity, of an infinite richness, superior to any that the intellect could dream of, for the intellect is only one of its aspects or products."

What a contrast to Herbert Spencer's view of life and evolution! "Life," says Spencer, "consists of inner action so adjusted as to balance outer action." True enough, no doubt, but not interesting. If the philosopher could tell us what it is that brings about the adjustment, and that profits by it, we should at once prick up our ears. Of course, it is life. But what is life? It is inner action so adjusted as to balance outer action!

A recent contemptuous critic of M. Bergson's book, Hugh S. R. Elliot, points out, as if he were triumphantly vindicating the physico-chemical theory of the nature and origin of life, what a complete machine a cabbage is for converting solar energy into chemical and vital energy - how it takes up the raw material from the soil by a chemical and mechanical process, how these are brought into contact with the light and air through the leaves, and thus the cabbage is built up. In like manner, a man is a machine for converting chemical energy derived from the food he eats into motion, and the like. As if M. Bergson, or any one else, would dispute these things! In the same way, a steam-engine is a machine for converting the energy latent in coal into motion and power; but what force lies back of the engine, and was active in the construction?

The final question of the cabbage and the man still remains - Where did you get them?

You assume vitality to start with - how did you get it? Did it arise spontaneously out of dead matter? Mechanical and chemical forces do all the work of the living body, but who or what controls and directs them, so that one compounding of the elements begets a cabbage, and another compounding of the same elements begets an oak - one mixture of them and we have a frog, another and we have a man? Is there not room here for something besides blind, indifferent forces? If we make the molecules themselves creative, then we are begging the question. The creative energy by any other name remains the same.

IV

If life itself is not a force or a form of energy, yet behold what energy it is capable of exerting! It seems to me that Sir Oliver Lodge is a little confusing when he says in a recent essay that "life does not exert force - not even the most microscopical force - and certainly does not supply energy." Sir Oliver is thinking of life as a distinct entity - something apart from the matter which it animates. But even in this case can we not say that the mainspring of the energy of living bodies is the life that is in them?

Apart from the force exerted by living animal bodies, see the force exerted by living plant bodies. I thought of the remark of Sir Oliver one day not long after reading it, while I was walking in a beech wood and noted how the sprouting beechnuts had sent their pale radicles down through the dry leaves upon which they were lying, often piercing two or three of them, and forcing their way down into the mingled soil and leaf-mould a couple of inches. Force was certainly expended in doing this, and if the life in the sprouting nut did not exert it or expend it, what did?

When I drive a peg into the ground with my axe or mallet, is the life in my arm any more strictly the source (the secondary source) of the energy expended than is the nut in this case? Of course, the sun is the primal source of the energy in both cases, and in all cases, but does not life exert the force, use it, bring it to bear, which it receives from the universal fount of energy?

Life cannot supply energy *de novo*, cannot create it out of nothing, but it can and must draw upon the store of energy in which the earth floats as in a sea. When this energy or force is manifest through a living body, we call it vital force; when it is manifest through a mechanical contrivance, we call it mechanical force; when it is developed by the action and reaction of chemical compounds, we call it chemical force; the same force in each case, but behaving so differently in the one case from what it does in the other that we come to think of it as a new and distinct entity. Now if Sir Oliver or any one else could tell us what force is, this difference between the vitalists and the mechanists might be reconciled.

Darwin measured the force of the downward growth of the radicle, such as I have alluded to, as one quarter of a pound, and its lateral pressure as much greater. We know that the roots of trees insert themselves into seams in the rocks, and force the parts asunder. This force is measurable and is often very great. Its seat seems to be in the soft, milky substance called the cambium layer under the bark. These minute cells when their force is combined may become regular rock-splitters.

One of the most remarkable exhibitions of plant force I ever saw was in a Western city where I observed a species of wild sunflower forcing its way up through the asphalt pavement; the folded and compressed leaves of the plant, like a man's fist, had pushed against the hard but flexible concrete till it had bulged up and then split, and let the irrepressible plant through. The force exerted must have been many pounds. I think it doubtful if the strongest man could have pushed his fist through such a resisting medium. If it was not life which exerted this force, what was it? Life activities are a kind of explosion, and the slow continued explosions of this growing plant rent the pavement as surely as powder would have done. It is doubtful if any cultivated plant could have overcome such odds. It required the force of the untamed hairy plant of the plains to accomplish this feat.

That life does not supply energy, that is, is not an independent source of energy, seems to me obvious enough, but that it does not manifest energy, use energy, or "exert force," is far from obvious. If a growing plant or tree does not exert force by reason of its growing, or by virtue of a specific kind of activity among its particles, which we name life, and which does not take place in a stone or in a bar of iron or in dead timber, then how can we say that any mechanical device or explosive compound exerts force? The steam-engine does not create force, neither does the exploding dynamite, but these things exert force. We have to think of the sum total of the force of the universe, as of matter itself, as a constant factor, that can neither be increased nor diminished. All activity, organic and inorganic, draws upon this force: the plant and tree, as well as the engine and the explosive - the winds, the tides, the animal, the vegetable alike. I can think of but one force, but of any number of manifestations of force, and of two distinct kinds of manifestations, the organic and the inorganic, or the vital and the physical, - the latter divisible into the chemical and the mechanical, the former made up of these two working in infinite complexity because drawn into new relations, and lifted to higher ends by this something we call life.

We think of something in the organic that lifts and moves and redistributes dead matter, and builds it up into the ten thousand new forms which it would never assume without this something; it lifts lime and iron and silica and potash and carbon, against gravity, up into trees and animal forms, not by a new force, but by an old force in the hands of a new agent.

The cattle move about the field, the drift boulders slowly creep down the slopes; there is no doubt that the final source of the force is in both cases the same; what we call gravity, a name for a mystery, is the form it takes in the case of the rocks, and what we call vitality, another name for a mystery, is the form it takes in the case of the cattle; without the solar and stellar energy, could there be any motion of either rock or beast?

Force is universal, it pervades all nature, one manifestation of it we call heat, another light, another electricity, another cohesion, chemical affinity, and so on. May not another manifestation of it be called life, differing from all the rest more radically than they differ from one another; bound up with all the rest and inseparable from them and identical with them only in its ultimate source in the Creative Energy that is immanent in the universe? I have to think of the Creative Energy as immanent in all matter, and the final source of all the transformations and transmutations we see in the organic and the inorganic worlds. The very nature of our minds compels us to postulate some power, or some principle, not as lying back of, but as active in, all the changing forms of life and nature, and their final source and cause.

The mind is satisfied when it finds a word that gives it a hold of a thing or a process, or when it can picture to itself just how the thing occurs. Thus, for instance, to account for the power generated by the rushing together of hydrogen and oxygen to produce water, we have to conceive of space between the atoms of these elements, and that the force generated comes from the immense velocity with which the infinitesimal atoms rush together across this infinitesimal space. It is quite possible that this is not the true explanation at all, but it satisfies the mind because it is an explanation in terms of mechanical forces that we know.

The solar energy goes into the atoms or corpuscles one thing, and it comes out another; it goes in as inorganic force, and it comes out as organic and psychic. The change or transformation takes place in those invisible laboratories of the infinitesimal atoms. It helps my mental processes to give that change a name - vitality - and to recognize it as a supramechanical force. Pasteur wanted a name for it and called it "dissymmetric force."

We are all made of one stuff undoubtedly, vegetable and animal, man and woman, dog and donkey, and the secret of the difference between us, and of the passing along of the difference from generation to generation with but slight variations, may be, so to speak, in the way the molecules and atoms of our bodies take hold of hands and perform their mystic dances in the inner temple of life. But one would like to know who or what pipes the tune and directs the figures of the dance.

In the case of the beechnuts, what is it that lies dormant in the substance of the nuts and becomes alive, under the influence of the warmth and moisture of spring, and puts out a radicle that pierces the dry leaves like an awl? The pebbles, though they contain the same chemical elements, do not become active and put out a radicle.

The chemico-physical explanation of the universe goes but a little way. These are the tools of the creative process, but they are not that process, nor its prime cause. Start the flame of life going, and the rest may be explained in terms of chemistry; start the human body developing, and physiological processes explain its growth; but why it becomes a man and not a monkey - what explains that?

II

THE LIVING WAVE

I

If one attempts to reach any rational conclusion on the question of the nature and origin of life on this planet, he soon finds himself in close quarters with two difficulties. He must either admit of a break in the course of nature and the introduction of a new principle, the vital principle, which, if he is a man of science, he finds it hard to do; or he must accept the theory of the physico-chemical origin of life, which, as a being with a soul, he finds it equally hard to do. In other words, he must either draw an arbitrary line between the inorganic and the organic when he knows that drawing arbitrary lines in nature, and fencing off one part from another, is an unscientific procedure, and one that often leads to bewildering contradictions; or he must look upon himself with all his high thoughts and aspirations, and upon all other manifestations of life, as merely a chance product of the blind mechanical and chemical action and interaction of the inorganic forces.

Either conclusion is distasteful. One does not like to think of himself as a chance hit of the irrational physical elements; neither does he feel at ease with the thought that he is the result of any break or discontinuity in natural law. He likes to see himself as vitally and inevitably related to the physical order as is the fruit to the tree that bore it, or the child to the mother that carried it in her womb, and yet, if only mechanical and chemical forces entered into his genesis, he does not feel himself well fathered and mothered.

One may evade the difficulty, as Helmholtz did, by regarding life as eternal - that it had no beginning in time; or, as some other German biologists have done, that the entire cosmos is alive and the earth a living organism.

If biogenesis is true, and always has been true, - no life without antecedent life, - then the question of a beginning is unthinkable. It is just as easy to think of a stick with only one end.

Such stanch materialists and mechanists as Haeckel and Verworn seem to have felt compelled, as a last resort, to postulate a psychic principle in nature, though of a low order. Haeckel says that most chemists and physicists will not hear a word about a "soul" in the atom. "In my opinion, however," he says, "in order to explain the simplest physical and chemical processes, we must necessarily assume a low order of psychical activity among the homogeneous particles of plasm, rising a very little above that of the crystal." In crystallization he sees a low degree of sensation and a little higher degree in the plasm.

Have we not in this rudimentary psychic principle which Haeckel ascribes to the atom a germ to start with that will ultimately give us the mind of man? With this spark, it seems to me, we can kindle a flame that will consume Haeckel's whole mechanical theory of creation. Physical science is clear that the non-living or inorganic world was before the living or organic world, but that the latter in some mysterious way lay folded in the former. Science has for many years been making desperate efforts to awaken this slumbering life in its laboratories, but has not yet succeeded, and probably never will succeed. Life without antecedent life seems a biological impossibility. The theory of spontaneous generation is rejected by the philosophical mind, because our experience tells us that everything has its antecedent, and that there is and can be no end to the causal sequences.

Spencer believes that the organic and inorganic fade into each other by insensible gradations - that no line can be drawn between them so that one can say, on this side is the organic, on that the inorganic. In other words, he says it is not necessary for us to think of an absolute commencement of organic life, or of a first organism - organic matter was not produced all at once, but was reached through steps or gradations. Yet it puzzles one to see how there can be any gradations or degrees between being and not being. Can there be any halfway house between something and nothing?

II

There is another way out of the difficulty that besets our rational faculties in their efforts to solve this question, and that is the audacious way of Henri Bergson in his "Creative Evolution." It is to deny any validity to the conclusion of our logical faculties upon this subject. Our intellect, Bergson says, cannot grasp the true nature of life, nor the meaning of the evolutionary movement. With the emphasis of italics he repeats that "*the intellect is characterized by a natural inability to comprehend life.*" He says this in a good many pages and in a good many different ways; the idea is one of the main conclusions of his book. Our intuitions, our spiritual nature, according to this philosopher, are more *en rapport* with the secrets of the creative energy than are our intellectual faculties; the key to the problem is to be found here, rather than in the mechanics and chemistry of the latter. Our intellectual faculties can grasp the physical order because they are formed by a world of solids and fluids and give us the power to deal with them and act upon them. But they cannot grasp the nature and the meaning of the vital order.

"We treat the living like the lifeless, and think all reality, however fluid, under the form of the sharply defined solid. We are at ease only in the discontinuous, in the immobile, in the dead. Perceiving in an organism only parts external to parts, the understanding has the choice between two systems of explanation only: either to regard the infinitely complex (and thereby infinitely well contrived) organization as a fortuitous concatenation of atoms, or to relate it to the incomprehensible influence of an external force that has grouped its elements together."

"Everything is obscure in the idea of creation, if we think of things which are created and a thing which creates." If we follow the lead of our logical, scientific faculties, then, we shall all be mechanists and materialists. Science can make no other solution of the problem because it sees from the outside. But if we look from the inside, with the spirit or "with that faculty of seeing which is immanent in the faculty of acting," we shall escape from the bondage of the mechanistic view into the freedom of the larger truth of the ceaseless creative view; we shall see the unity of the creative impulse which is immanent in life and which, "passing through generations, links individuals with individuals, species with species, and makes of the whole series of the living one single immense wave flowing over matter."

I recall that Tyndall, who was as much poet as scientist, speaks of life as a wave "which at no two consecutive moments of its existence is composed of the same particles." In his more sober scientific mood Tyndall would doubtless have rejected M. Bergson's view of life, yet his image of the wave is very Bergsonian. But what different meanings the two writers aim to convey: Tyndall is thinking of the fact that a living body is constantly taking up new material on the one side and dropping dead or outworn material on the other. M. Bergson's mind is occupied with the thought of the primal push or impulsion of matter which travels through it as the force in the wave traverses the water. The wave embodies a force which lifts the water up in opposition to its tendency to seek and keep a level, and travels on, leaving the water behind. So does this something we call life break the deadlock of inert matter and lift it into a thousand curious and beautiful forms, and then, passing on, lets it fall back again into a state of dead equilibrium.

Tyndall was one of the most eloquent exponents of the materialistic theory of the origin of life, and were he living now would probably feel little or no sympathy with the Bergsonian view of a primordial life impulse. He found the key to all life phenomena in the hidden world of molecular attraction and repulsion. He says: "Molecular forces determine the form which the solar energy will assume. [What a world of mystery lies in that determinism of the hidden molecular forces!] In the separation of the carbon and oxygen this energy may be so conditioned as to result in one case in the formation of a cabbage and in another case in the formation of an oak. So also as regards the reunion of the carbon and the oxygen [in the animal organism] the molecular machinery through which the combining energy acts may in one case weave the texture of a frog, while in another it may weave the texture of a man."

But is not this molecular force itself a form of solar energy, and can it differ in kind from any other form of physical force? If molecular forces determine whether the solar energy shall weave a head of a cabbage or a head of a Plato or a Shakespeare, does it not meet all the requirements of our conception of creative will?

Tyndall thinks that a living man - Socrates, Aristotle, Goethe, Darwin, I suppose - could be produced directly from inorganic nature in the laboratory if (and note what a momentous "if" this is) we could put together the elements of such a man in the same relative positions as those which they occupy in his body, "with the selfsame forces and distribution of forces, the selfsame motions and distribution of motions." Do this and you have a St. Paul or a Luther or a Lincoln. Dr. Verworn said essentially the same thing in a lecture before one of our colleges while in this country a few years ago - easy enough to manufacture a living being of any order of intellect if you can reproduce in the laboratory his "internal and external *vital conditions*." (The italics are mine.) To produce those vital conditions is where the rub comes. Those vital conditions, as regards the minutest bit of protoplasm, science, with all her tremendous resources, has not yet been able to produce. The raising of Lazarus from the dead seems no more a miracle than evoking vital conditions in dead matter. External and internal vital conditions are no doubt inseparably correlated, and when we can produce them we shall have life. Life, says Verworn, is like fire, and "is a phenomenon of nature which appears as soon as the complex of its conditions is fulfilled." We can easily produce fire by mechanical and chemical means, but not life. Fire is a chemical process, it is rapid oxidation, and oxidation is a disintegrating process, while life is an integrating process, or a balance maintained between the two by what we call the vital force. Life is evidently a much higher form of molecular activity than combustion. The old Greek Heraclitus saw, and the modern scientist sees, very superficially in comparing the two.

I have no doubt that Huxley was right in his inference "that if the properties of matter result from the nature and disposition of its component molecules, then there is no intelligible ground for refusing to say that the properties of protoplasm result from the nature and disposition of its molecules." It is undoubtedly in that nature and disposition of the biological molecules that Tyndall's whole "mystery and miracle of vitality" is wrapped up. If we could only grasp what it is that transforms the molecule of dead matter into the living molecule! Pasteur called it "dissymmetric force," which is only a new name for the mystery. He believed there was an "irrefragable physical barrier between organic and inorganic nature" - that the molecules of an organism differed from those of a mineral, and for this difference he found a name.

III

There seems to have been of late years a marked reaction, even among men of science, from the mechanistic conception of life as held by the band of scientists to which I have referred. Something like a new vitalism is making headway both on the Continent and in Great Britain. Its exponents urge that biological problems "defy any attempt at a mechanical explanation." These men stand for the idea "of the creative individuality of organisms" and that the main factors in organic evolution cannot be accounted for by the forces already operative in the inorganic world.

There is, of course, a mathematical chance that in the endless changes and permutations of inert matter the four principal elements that make up a living body may fall or run together in just that order and number that the kindling of the flame of life requires, but it is a disquieting proposition. One atom too much or too little of any of them, - three of oxygen where two were required, or two of nitrogen where only one was wanted, - and the face of the world might have been vastly different. Not only did much depend on their coming together, but upon the order of their coming; they must unite in just such an order. Insinuate an atom or corpuscle of hydrogen or carbon at the wrong point in the ranks, and the trick is a failure. Is there any chance that they will hit upon a combination of things and forces that will make a machine - a watch, a gun, or even a row of pins?

When we regard all the phenomena of life and the spell it seems to put upon inert matter, so that it behaves so differently from the same matter before it is drawn into the life circuit, when we see how it lifts up a world of dead particles out of the soil against gravity into trees and animals; how it changes the face of the earth; how it comes and goes while matter stays; how it defies chemistry and physics to evoke it from the non-living; how its departure, or cessation, lets the matter fall back to the inorganic - when we consider these and others like them, we seem compelled to think of life as something, some force or principle in itself, as M. Bergson and Sir Oliver Lodge do, existing apart from the matter it animates.

Sir Oliver Lodge, famous physicist that he is, yet has a vein of mysticism and idealism in him which sometimes makes him recoil from the hard-and-fast interpretations of natural phenomena by physical science. Like M. Bergson, he sees in life some tendency or impetus which arose in matter at a definite time and place, "and which has continued to interact with and incarnate itself in matter ever since."

If a living body is a machine, then we behold a new kind of machine with new kinds of mechanical principles - a machine that repairs itself, that reproduces itself, a clock that winds itself up, an engine that stokes itself, a gun that aims itself, a machine that divides and makes two, two unite and make four, a million or more unite and make a man or a tree - a machine that is nine tenths water, a machine that feeds on other machines, a machine that grows stronger with use; in fact, a machine that does all sorts of unmechanical things and that no known combination of mechanical and chemical principles can reproduce - a vital machine. The idea of the vital as something different from and opposed to the mechanical must come in. Something had to be added to the mechanical and chemical to make the vital.

Spencer explains in terms of physics why an ox is larger than the sheep, but he throws no light upon the subject of the individuality of these animals - what it is that makes an ox an ox or a sheep a sheep. These animals are built up out of the same elements by the same processes, and they may both have had the same stem form in remote biologic time. If so, what made them diverge and develop into such totally different forms? After the living body is once launched many, if not all, of its operations and economies can be explained on principles of mechanics and chemistry, but the something that avails itself of these principles and develops an ox in the one case and a sheep in the other - what of that?

Spencer is forced into using the terms "amount of vital capital." How much more of it some men, some animals, some plants have than others! What is it? What did Spencer mean by it? This capital augments from youth to manhood, and then after a short or long state of equilibrium slowly declines to the vanishing-point.

Again, what a man does depends upon what he is, and what he is depends upon what he does. Structure determines function, and function reacts upon structure. This interaction goes on throughout life; cause and effect interchange or play into each other's hands. The more power we spend within limits the more power we have. This is another respect in which life is utterly unmechanical. A machine does not grow stronger by use as our muscles do; it does not store up or conserve the energy it expends. The gun is weaker by every ball it hurls; not so the baseball pitcher; he is made stronger up to the limit of his capacity for strength.

It is plain enough that all living beings are machines in this respect - they are kept going by the reactions between their interior and their exterior; these reactions are either mechanical, as in flying, swimming, walking, and involve gravitation, or they are chemical and assimilative, as in breathing and eating. To that extent all living things are machines - some force exterior to themselves must aid in keeping them going; there is no spontaneous or uncaused movement in them; and yet what a difference between a machine and a living thing!

True it is that a man cannot live and function without heat and oxygen, nor long without food, and yet his relation to his medium and environment is as radically different from that of the steam-engine as it is possible to express. His driving-wheel, the heart, acts in response to some stimulus as truly as does the piston of the engine, and the principles involved in circulation are all mechanical; and yet the main thing is not mechanical, but vital. Analyze the vital activities into principles of mechanics and of chemistry, if you will, yet there is something involved that is neither mechanical nor chemical, though it may be that only the imagination can grasp it.

The type that prints the book is set up and again distributed by a purely mechanical process, but that which the printed page signifies involves something not mechanical. The mechanical and chemical principles operative in men's bodies are all the same; the cell structure is the same, and yet behold the difference between men in size, in strength, in appearance, in temperament, in disposition, in capacities! All the processes of respiration, circulation, and nutrition in our bodies involve well-known mechanical principles, and the body is accurately described as a machine; and yet if there were not something in it that transcends mechanics and chemistry would you and I be here? A machine is the same whether it is in action or repose, but when a body ceases to function, it is not the same. It cannot be set going like a machine; the motor power has ceased to be. But if the life of the body were no more than the sum of the reactions existing between the body and the medium in which it lives, this were not so. A body lives as long as there is a proper renewal of the interior medium through exchanges with its environment.

Mechanical principles are operative in every part of the body - in the heart, in the arteries, in the limbs, in the joints, in the bowels, in the muscles; and chemical principles are operative in the lungs, in the stomach, in the liver, in the kidneys; but to all these things do we not have to add something that is not mechanical or chemical to make the man, to make the plant? A higher mechanics, a higher chemistry, if you prefer, a force, but a force differing in kind from the physical forces.

The forces of life are constructive forces, and work in a world of disintegrating or destructive forces which oppose them and which they overcome. The mechanical and the chemical forces of dead matter are the enemies of the forces of life till life overcomes and uses them; as much so as gravity, fire, frost, water are man's enemies till he has learned how to subdue and use them.

IV

It is a significant fact that the four chief elements which in various combinations make up living bodies are by their extreme mobility well suited to their purpose. Three of these are gaseous; only the carbon is a solid. This renders them facile and adaptive in the ever-changing conditions of organic evolution. The solid carbon forms the vessel in which the precious essence of life is carried. Without carbon we should evaporate or flow away and escape. Much of the oxygen and hydrogen enters into living bodies as water; nine tenths of the human body is water; a little nitrogen and a few mineral salts make up the rest. So that our life in its final elements is little more than a stream of water holding in solution carbonaceous and other matter and flowing, forever flowing, a stream of fluid and solid matter plus something else that scientific analysis cannot reach - some force or principle that combines and organizes these elements into the living body.

If a man could be reduced instantly into his constituent elements we should see a pail or two of turbid fluid that would flow down the bank and soon be lost in the soil. That which gives us our form and stability and prevents us from slowly spilling down the slope at all times is the mysterious vital principle or force which knits and marries these unstable elements together and raises up a mobile but more or less stable form out of the world of fluids. Venus rising from the sea is a symbol of the genesis of every living thing.

Inorganic matter seeks only rest. "Let me alone," it says; "do not break my slumbers." But as soon as life awakens in it, it says: "Give me room, get out of my way. Ceaseless activity, ceaseless change, a thousand new forms are what I crave." As soon as life enters matter, matter meets with a change of heart. It is lifted to another plane, the supermechanical plane; it behaves in a new way; its movements from being calculable become incalculable. A straight line has direction, that is mechanics; what direction has the circle? That is life, a change of direction every instant. An aeroplane is built entirely on mechanical principles, but something not so built has to sit in it and guide it; in fact, had to build it and adjust it to its end.

Mechanical forces seek an equilibrium or a state of rest. The whole inorganic world under the influence of gravity would flow as water flows, if it could, till it reached a state of absolute repose. But vital forces struggle against a state of repose, which to them means death. They are vital by virtue of their tendency to resist the repose of inert matter; chemical activity disintegrates a stone or other metal, but the decay of organized matter is different in kind; living organisms decompose it and resolve it into its original compounds.

Vital connections and mechanical connections differ in kind. You can treat mechanical principles mathematically, but can you treat life mathematically? Will your formulas and equations apply here? You can figure out the eclipses of the sun and moon for centuries to come, but who can figure out the eclipses of nations or the overthrow of parties or the failures of great men? And it is not simply because the problem is so vastly more complex; it is because you are in a world where mathematical principles do not apply. Mechanical forces will determine the place and shape of every particle of inert matter any number of years or centuries hence, but they will not determine the place and condition of matter imbued with the principle of life.

We can graft living matter, we can even graft a part of one animal's body into another animal's body, but the mechanical union which we bring about must be changed into vital union to be a success, the spirit of the body has to second our efforts. The same in grafting a tree or anything else: the mechanical union which we effect must become a vital union; and this will not take place without some degree of consanguinity, the live scion must be recognized and adapted by the stock in which we introduce it.

Living matter may be symbolized by a stream; it is ever and

never the same; life is a constant becoming; our minds and our bodies are never the same at any two moments of time; life is ceaseless change.

No doubt it is between the stable and the unstable condition of the molecules of matter that life is born. The static condition to which all things tend is death. Matter in an unstable condition tends either to explode or to grow or to disintegrate. So that an explosion bears some analogy to life, only it is quickly over and the static state of the elements is restored. Life is an infinitely slower explosion, or a prolonged explosion, during which some matter of the organism is being constantly burned up, and thus returned to a state of inorganic repose, while new matter is taken in and kindled and consumed by the fires of life. One can visualize all this and make it tangible to the intellect. Get your fire of life started and all is easy, but how to start it is the rub. Get your explosive compound, and something must break the deadlock of the elements before it will explode. So in life, what is it that sets up this slow gentle explosion that makes the machinery of our vital economies go - that draws new matter into the vortex and casts the used-up material out - in short, that creates and keeps up the unstable condition, the seesaw upon which life depends? To enable the mind to grasp it we have to invent or posit some principle, call it the vital force, as so many have done and still do, or call it molecular force, as Tyndall does, or the power of God, as our orthodox brethren do, it matters not. We are on the border-land between the knowable and the unknowable, where the mind can take no further step. There is no life without carbon and oxygen, hydrogen and nitrogen, but there is a world of these elements without life. What must be added to them to set up the reaction we call life? Nothing that chemistry can disclose.

New tendencies and activities are set up among these elements, but the elements themselves are not changed; oxygen is still oxygen and carbon still carbon, yet behold the wonder of their new workmanship under the tutelage of life!

Life only appears when the stable passes into the unstable, yet this change takes place all about us in our laboratories, and no life appears. We can send an electric spark through a room full of oxygen and hydrogen gas, and with a tremendous explosion we have water - an element of life, but not life.

Some of the elements seem nearer life than others. Water is near life; heat, light, the colloid state are near life; osmosis, oxidation, chemical reactions are near life; the ashes of inorganic bodies are nearer life than the same minerals in the rocks and soil; but none of these things is life.

The chemical mixture of some of the elements gives us our high explosives - gunpowder, guncotton, and the like; their organic mixture gives a slower kind of explosive - bread, meat, milk, fruit, which, when acted upon by the vital forces of the body, yield the force that is the equivalent of the work the body does. But to combine them in the laboratory so as to produce the compounds out of which the body can extract force is impossible. We can make an unstable compound that will hurl a ton of iron ten miles, but not one that when exploded in the digestive tract of the human body will lift a hair.

We may follow life down to the ground, yes, under the ground, into the very roots of matter and motion, yea, beyond the roots, into the imaginary world of molecules and atoms, and their attractions and repulsions and not find its secret. Indeed, science - the new science - pursues matter to the vanishing-point, where it ceases to become matter and becomes pure force or spirit. What takes place in that imaginary world where ponderable matter ends and becomes disembodied force, and where the hypothetical atoms are no longer divisible, we may conjecture but may never know. We may fancy the infinitely little going through a cycle of evolution like that of the infinitely great, and solar systems developing and revolving inside of the ultimate atoms, but the Copernicus or the Laplace of the atomic astronomy has not yet appeared. The atom itself is an invention of science. To get the mystery of vitality reduced to the atom is getting it in very close quarters, but it is a very big mystery still. Just how the dead becomes alive, even in the atom, is mystery enough to stagger any scientific mind. It is not the volume of the change; it is the quality or kind. Chemistry and mechanics we have always known, and they always remain chemistry and mechanics. They go into our laboratories and through our devices chemistry and mechanics, and they come out chemistry and mechanics. They will never come out life, conjure with them as we will, and we can get no other result. We cannot inaugurate the mystic dance among the atoms that will give us the least throb of life.

The psychic arises out of the organic and the organic arises out of the inorganic, and the inorganic arises out of - what? The relation of each to the other is as intimate as that of the soul to the body; we cannot get between them even in thought, but the difference is one of kind and not of degree. The vital transcends the mechanical, and the psychic transcends the vital - is on another plane, and yet without the sun's energy there could be neither. Thus are things knit together; thus does one thing flow out of or bloom out of another. We date from the rocks, and the rocks date from the fiery nebulae, and the loom in which the texture of our lives was woven is the great loom of vital energy about us and in us; but what hand guided the shuttle and invented the pattern - who knows?

III

A WONDERFUL WORLD

I

Science recognizes a more fundamental world than that of matter. This is the electro-magnetic world which underlies the material world and which, as Professor Soddy says, probably completely embraces it, and has no mechanical analogy. To those accustomed only to the grosser ideas of matter and its motions, says the British scientist, this electro-magnetic world is as difficult to conceive of as it would be for us to walk upon air. Yet many times in our lives is this world in overwhelming evidence before us. During a thunderstorm we get an inkling of how fearfully and wonderfully the universe in which we live is made, and what energy and activity its apparent passivity and opacity mark. A flash of lightning out of a storm-cloud seems instantly to transform the whole passive universe into a terrible living power. This slow, opaque, indifferent matter about us and above us, going its silent or noisy round of mechanical and chemical change, ponderable, insensate, obstructive, slumbering in the rocks, quietly active in the soil, gently rustling in the trees, sweetly purling in the brooks, slowly, invisibly building and shaping our bodies - how could we ever dream that it held in leash such a terrible, ubiquitous, spectacular thing as this of the forked lightning? If we were to see and hear it for the first time, should we not think that the Judgment Day had really come? that the great seals of the

Book of Fate were being broken?

What an awakening it is! what a revelation! what a fearfully dramatic actor suddenly leaps upon the stage! Had we been permitted to look behind the scenes, we could not have found him; he was not there, except potentially; he was born and equipped in a twinkling. One stride, and one word which shakes the house, and he is gone; gone as quickly as he came. Look behind the curtain and he is not there. He has vanished more completely than any stage ghost ever vanished - he has withdrawn into the innermost recesses of the atomic structure of matter, and is diffused through the clouds, to be called back again, as the elemental drama proceeds, as suddenly as before.

All matter is charged with electricity, either actual or potential; the sun is hot with it, and doubtless our own heart-beats, our own thinking brains, are intimately related to it; yet it is palpable and visible only in this sudden and extraordinary way. It defies our analysis, it defies our definitions; it is inscrutable and incomprehensible, yet it will do our errands, light our houses, cook our dinners, and pull our loads.

How humdrum and constant and prosaic the other forces - gravity, cohesion, chemical affinity, and capillary attraction - seem when compared with this force of forces, electricity! How deep and prolonged it slumbers at one time, how terribly active and threatening at another, bellowing through the heavens like an infuriated god seeking whom he may destroy!

The warring of the elements at such times is no figure of speech. What has so disturbed the peace in the electric equilibrium, as to make possible this sudden outburst, this steep incline in the stream of energy, this ethereal Niagara pouring from heaven to earth? Is a thunderstorm a display of the atomic energy of which the physicists speak, and which, were it available for our use, would do all the work of the world many times over?

How marvelous that the softest summer breeze, or the

impalpable currents of the calmest day, can be torn asunder with such suddenness and violence, by the accumulated energy that slumbers in the imaginary atoms, as to give forth a sound like the rending of mountains or the detonations of earthquakes!

Electricity is the soul of matter. If Whitman's paradox is true, that the soul and body are one, in the same sense the scientific paradox is true: that matter and electricity are one, and both are doubtless a phase of the universal ether - a reality which can be described only in terms of the negation of matter. In a flash of lightning we see pure disembodied energy - probably that which is the main-spring of the universe. Modern science is more and more inclined to find the explanation of all vital phenomena in electrical stress and change. We know that an electric current will bring about chemical changes otherwise impracticable. Nerve force, if not a form of electricity, is probably inseparable from it. Chemical changes equivalent to the combustion of fuel and the corresponding amount of available energy released have not yet been achieved outside of the living body without great loss. The living body makes a short cut from fuel to energy, and this avoids the wasteful process of the engine. What part electricity plays in this process is, of course, only conjectural.

II

Our daily lives go on for the most part in two worlds, the world of mechanical transposition and the world of chemical transformations, but we are usually conscious only of the former. This is the visible, palpable world of motion and change that rushes and roars around us in the winds, the storms, the floods, the moving and falling bodies, and the whole panorama of our material civilization; the latter is the world of silent, invisible, unsleeping, and all-potent chemical reactions that take place all about us and is confined to the atoms and molecules of matter, as the former is confined to its visible aggregates.

Mechanical forces and chemical affinities rule our physical lives, and indirectly our psychic lives as well. When we come into the world and draw our first breath, mechanics and chemistry start us on our career. Breathing is a mechanical, or a mechanico-vital, act; the mechanical principle involved is the same as that involved in the working of a bellows, but the oxidation of the blood when the air enters the lungs is a chemical act, or a chemico-vital act. The air gives up a part of its oxygen, which goes into the arterial circulation, and its place is taken by carbonic-acid gas and watery vapor. The oxygen feeds and keeps going the flame of life, as literally as it feeds and keeps going the fires in our stoves and furnaces.

Hence our most constant and vital relation to the world without is a chemical one. We can go without food for some days, but we can exist without breathing only a few moments. Through these spongy lungs of ours we lay hold upon the outward world in the most intimate and constant way. Through them we are rooted to the air. The air is a mechanical mixture of two very unlike gases - nitrogen and oxygen; one very inert, the other very active. Nitrogen is like a cold-blooded, lethargic person - it combines with other substances very reluctantly and with but little energy. Oxygen is just its opposite in this respect: it gives itself freely; it is "Hail, fellow;

well met!" with most substances, and it enters into co-partnership with them on such a large scale that it forms nearly one half of the material of the earth's crust. This invisible gas, this breath of air, through the magic of chemical combination, forms nearly half the substance of the solid rocks. Deprive it of its affinity for carbon, or substitute nitrogen or hydrogen in its place, and the air would quickly suffocate us. That changing of the dark venous blood in our lungs into the bright, red, arterial blood would instantly cease. Fancy the sensation of inhaling an odorless, non-poisonous atmosphere that would make one gasp for breath! We should be quickly poisoned by the waste of our own bodies. All things that live must have oxygen, and all things that burn must have oxygen. Oxygen does not burn, but it supports combustion.

And herein is one of the mysteries of chemistry again. This support which the oxygen gives is utterly unlike any support we are acquainted with in the world of mechanical forces. Oxygen supports combustion by combining chemically with carbon, and the evolution of heat and light is the result. And this is another mystery - this chemical union which takes place in the ultimate particles of matter and which is so radically different from a mechanical mixture. In a chemical union the atoms are not simply in juxtaposition; they are, so to speak, inside of one another - each has swallowed another and lost its identity, an impossible feat, surely, viewed in the light of our experiences with tangible bodies. In the visible, mechanical world no two bodies can occupy the same place at the same time, but apparently in chemistry they can and do. An atom of oxygen and one of carbon, or of hydrogen, unite and are lost in each other; it is a marriage wherein the two or three become one. In dealing with the molecules and atoms of matter we are in a world wherein the laws of solid bodies do not apply; friction is abolished, elasticity is perfect, and place and form play no part. We have escaped from matter as we know it, the solid, fluid, or gaseous forms, and are dealing with it in its fourth or ethereal estate. In breathing, the oxygen goes into the blood, not to stay there, but to unite with and bring away the waste of the system in the shape of carbon, and re-enter the air again as one of the elements of carbonic-acid gas, CO_2. Then the reverse process takes place in the vegetable world, the leaves breathe this poisonous gas, release the oxygen under the chemistry of the sun's rays, and appropriate and store up the carbon. Thus do the animal and vegetable worlds play into each other's hands. The animal is dependent upon the vegetable for its carbon, which it releases again, through the life processes, as carbonic-acid gas, to be again drawn into the cycle of vegetable life.

The act of breathing well illustrates our mysterious relations to Nature - the cunning way in which she plays the principal part in our lives without our knowledge. How certain we are that we draw the air into our lungs - that we seize hold of it in some way as if it were a continuous substance, and pull it into our bodies! Are we not also certain that the pump sucks the water up through the pipe, and that we suck our iced drinks through a straw? We are quite unconscious of the fact that the weight of the superincumbent air does it all, that breathing is only to a very limited extent a voluntary act. It is controlled by muscular machinery, but that machinery would not act in a vacuum. We contract the diaphragm, or the diaphragm contracts under stimuli received through the medulla oblongata from those parts of the body which constantly demand oxygen, and a vacuum tends to form in the chest, which is constantly prevented by the air rushing in to fill it. The expansive force of the air under its own weight causes the lungs to fill, just as it causes the bellows of the blacksmith to fill when he works the lever, and the water to rise in the pump when we force out the air by working the handle. Another unconscious muscular effort under the influence of nerve stimulus, and the air is forced out of the lungs, charged with the bodily waste which it is the function to relieve. But the wonder of it all is how slight a part our wills play in the process, and how our lives are kept going by a mechanical force from without, seconded or supplemented by chemical and vital forces from within.

The one chemical process with which we are familiar all our lives, but which we never think of as such, is fire. Here on our own hearthstones goes on this wonderful spectacular and beneficent transformation of matter and energy, and yet we are grown so familiar with it that it moves us not. We can describe combustion in terms of chemistry, just as we can describe the life-processes in similar terms, yet the mystery is no more cleared up in the one case than in the other. Indeed, it seems to me that next to the mystery of life is the mystery of fire. The oxidizing processes are identical, only one is a building up or integrating process, and the other is a pulling down or disintegrating process. More than that, we can evoke fire any time, by both mechanical and chemical means, from the combustible matter about us; but we cannot evoke life. The equivalents of life do not slumber in our tools as do the equivalents of fire. Hence life is the deeper mystery. The ancients thought of a spirit of fire as they did of a spirit of health and of disease, and of good and bad spirits all about them, and as we think of a spirit of life, or of a creative life principle. Are we as wide of the mark as they were? So think many earnest students of living things. When we do not have to pass the torch of life along, but can kindle it in our laboratories, then this charge will assume a different aspect.

III

Nature works with such simple means! A little more or a little less of this or that, and behold the difference! A little more or a little less heat, and the face of the world is changed.

> "And the little more, and how much it is,
> And the little less, and what worlds away!"

At one temperature water is solid, at another it is fluid, at another it is a visible vapor, at a still higher it is an invisible vapor that burns like a flame. All possible shades of color lurk in a colorless ray of light. A little more or a little less heat makes all the difference between a nebula and a sun, and between a sun and a planet. At one degree of heat the elements are dissociated; at a lower degree they are united. At one point in the scale of temperatures life appears; at another it disappears. With heat enough the earth would melt like a snowball in a furnace, with still more it would become a vapor and float away like a cloud. More or less heat only makes the difference between the fluidity of water and the solidity of the rocks that it beats against, or of the banks that hold it.

The physical history of the universe is written in terms of heat and motion. Astronomy is the story of cooling suns and worlds. At a low enough temperature all chemical activity ceases. In our own experience we find that frost will blister like flame. In the one case heat passes into the tissues so quickly and in such quantity that a blister ensues; in the other, heat is abstracted so quickly and in such quantity that a like effect is produced. In one sense, life is a thermal phenomenon; so are all conditions of fluids and solids thermal phenomena.

Great wonders Nature seems to achieve by varying the arrangement of the same particles. Arrange or unite the atoms of carbon in one way and you have charcoal; assemble the same atoms in another order, and you have the diamond. The difference between the pearl and the oyster-shell that holds it is one of structure or arrangement of the same particles of matter. Arrange the atoms of silica in one way and you have a quartz pebble, in another way and you have a precious stone. The chemical constituents of alcohol and ether are the same; the difference in their qualities and properties arises from the way the elements are compounded - the way they take hold of hands, so to speak, in that marriage ceremony which constitutes a chemical compound. Compounds identical in composition and in molecular formulae may yet differ widely in physical properties; the elements are probably grouped in different ways, the atoms of carbon or of hydrogen probably carry different amounts of potential energy, so that the order in which they stand related to one another accounts for the different properties of the same chemical compounds. Different groupings of the same atoms of any of the elements result in a like difference of physical properties.

The physicists tell us that what we call the qualities of things, and their structure and composition, are but the expressions of internal atomic movements. A complex substance simply means a whirl, an intricate dance, of which chemical composition, histological structure, and gross configuration are the figures. How the atoms take hold of hands, as it were, the way they face, the poses they assume, the speed of their gyrations, the partners they exchange, determine the kinds of phenomena we are dealing with.

There is a striking analogy between the letters of our alphabet and their relation to the language of the vast volume of printed books, and the eighty or more primary elements and their relation to the vast universe of material things. The analogy may not be in all respects a strictly true one, but it is an illuminating one. Our twenty-six letters combined and repeated in different orders give us the many thousand words our language possesses, and these words combined and repeated in different orders give us the vast body of printed books in our libraries. The ultimate parts - the atoms and molecules of all literature, so to speak - are the letters of the alphabet. How often by changing a letter in a word, by reversing their order, or by substituting one letter for another, we get a word of an entirely different meaning, as in umpire and empire, petrifaction and putrefaction, malt and salt, tool and fool. And by changing the order of the words in a sentence we express all the infinite variety of ideas and meanings that the books of the world hold.

The eighty or more primordial elements are Nature's alphabet with which she writes her "infinite book of secrecy." Science shows pretty conclusively that the character of the different substances, their diverse qualities and properties, depend upon the order in which the atoms and molecules are combined. Change the order in which the molecules of the carbon and oxygen are combined in alcohol, and we get ether - the chemical formula remaining the same. Or take ordinary spirits of wine and add four more atoms of carbon to the carbon molecules, and we have the poison, carbolic acid. Pure alcohol is turned into a deadly poison by taking from it one atom of carbon and two of hydrogen. With the atoms of carbon, hydrogen, and oxygen, by combining them in different proportions and in different orders, Nature produces such diverse bodies as acetic acid, alcohol, sugar, starch, animal fats, vegetable oils, glycerine, and the like. So with the long list of hydrocarbons - gaseous, liquid, and solid - called paraffins, that are obtained from petroleum and that are all composed of hydrogen and carbon, but with a different number of atoms of each, like a different number of a's or b's or c's in a word.

What an enormous number of bodies Nature forms out of oxygen by uniting it chemically with other primary elements! Thus by uniting it with the element silica she forms half of the solid crust of the globe; by uniting it with hydrogen in the proportion of two to one she forms all the water of the globe. With one atom of nitrogen united chemically with three atoms of hydrogen she forms ammonia. With one atom of carbon united with four atoms of hydrogen she spells marsh gas; and so on. Carbon occurs in inorganic nature in two crystalline forms, - the diamond and black lead, or graphite, - their physical differences evidently being the result of their different molecular structure. Graphite is a good conductor of heat and electricity, and the diamond is not. Carbon in the organic world, where it plays such an important part, is non-crystalline. Under the influence of life its molecules are differently put together, as in sugar, starch, wood, charcoal, etc. There are also two forms of phosphorus, but not two kinds; the same atoms are probably united differently in each. The yellow waxy variety has such an affinity for oxygen that it will burn in water, and it is poisonous. Bring this variety to a high temperature away from the air, and its molecular structure seems to change, and we have the red variety, which is tasteless, odorless, and non-poisonous, and is not affected by contact with the air. Such is the mystery of chemical change.

IV

Science has developed methods and implements of incredible delicacy. Its "microbalance" can estimate "the difference of weight of the order of the millionth of a milligram." Light travels at the speed of 186,000 miles a second, yet science can follow it with its methods, and finds that it travels faster with the current of running water than against it. Science has perfected a thermal instrument by which it can detect the heat of a lighted candle six miles away, and the warmth of the human face several miles distant. It has devised a method by which it can count the particles in the alpha rays of radium that move at a velocity of twenty thousand kilometers a second, and a method by which, through the use of a screen of zinc-sulphide, it can see the flashes produced by the alpha atoms when they strike this screen. It weighs and counts and calculates the motions of particles of matter so infinitely small that only the imagination can grasp them. Its theories require it to treat the ultimate particles into which it resolves matter, and which are so small that they are no longer divisible, as if they were solid bodies with weight and form, with centre and circumference, colliding with one another like billiard-balls, or like cosmic bodies in the depths of space, striking one another squarely, and, for aught I know, each going through another, or else grazing one another and glancing off. To particles of matter so small that they can no longer be divided or made smaller, the impossible feat of each going through the centre of another, or of each enveloping the other, might be affirmed of them without adding to their unthinkableness. The theory is that if we divide a molecule of water the parts are no longer water, but atoms of hydrogen and oxygen - real bodies with weight and form, and storehouses of energy, but no longer divisible.

Indeed, the atomic theory of matter leads us into a non-material world, or a world the inverse of the solid, three-dimensioned world that our senses reveal to us, or to matter in a fourth estate. We know solids and fluids and gases; but emanations which are neither we know only as we know spirits and ghosts - by dreams or hearsay. Yet this fourth or ethereal estate of matter seems to be the final, real, and fundamental condition.

How it differs from spirit is not easy to define. The beta ray of radium will penetrate solid iron a foot thick, a feat that would give a spirit pause. The ether of space, which science is coming more and more to look upon as the mother-stuff of all things, has many of the attributes of Deity. It is omnipresent and all-powerful. Neither time nor space has dominion over it. It is the one immutable and immeasurable thing in the universe. From it all things arise and to it they return. It is everywhere and nowhere. It has none of the finite properties of matter - neither parts, form, nor dimension; neither density nor tenuity; it cannot be compressed nor expanded nor moved; it has no inertia nor mass, and offers no resistance; it is subject to no mechanical laws, and no instrument or experiment that science has yet devised can detect its presence; it has neither centre nor circumference, neither extension nor boundary. And yet science is as convinced of its existence as of the solid ground beneath our feet. It is the one final reality in the universe, if we may not say that it is the universe. Tremors or vibrations in it reach the eye and make an impression that we call light; electrical oscillations in it are the source of other phenomena. It is the fountain-head of all potential energy. The ether is an invention of the scientific imagination. We had to have it to account for light, gravity, and the action of one body upon another at a distance, as well as to account for other phenomena. The ether is not a body, it is a medium. All bodies are in motion; matter moves; the ether is in a state of absolute rest. Says Sir Oliver Lodge, "The ether is strained, and has the property of exerting strain and recoil." An electron is like a knot in the ether. The ether is the fluid of fluids, yet its tension or strain is so great that it is immeasurably more dense than anything else - a phenomenon that may be paralleled by a jet of water at such speed that it cannot be cut with a sword or severed by a hammer. It is so subtle or imponderable that solid bodies are as vacuums to it, and so pervasive that all conceivable space is filled with it; "so full," says Clerk Maxwell, "that no human power can remove it from the smallest portion of space, or produce the slightest flaw in its infinite continuity."

The scientific imagination, in its attempts to master the workings of the material universe, has thus given us a creation which in many of its attributes rivals Omnipotence. It is the sum of all contradictions, and the source of all reality. The gross matter which we see and feel is one state of it; electricity, which is without form and void, is another state of it; and our minds and souls, Sir Oliver Lodge intimates, may be still another state of it. But all these theories of physical science are justified by their fruits. The atomic theory of matter, and the kinetic theory of gases, are mathematically demonstrated. However unreal and fantastic they may appear to our practical faculties, conversant only with ponderable bodies, they bear the test of the most rigid and exact experimentation.

V

After we have marveled over all these hidden things, and been impressed by the world within world of the material universe, do we get any nearer to the mystery of life? Can we see where the tremendous change from the non-living to the living takes place? Can we evoke life from the omnipotent ether, or see it arise in the whirling stream of atoms and electrons? Molecular science opens up to us a world where the infinitely little matches the infinitely great, where matter is dematerialized and answers to many of the conceptions of spirit; but does it bring us any nearer the origin of life? Is radio-active matter any nearer living matter than is the clod under foot? Are the darting electrons any more vital than the shooting-stars? Can a flash of radium emanations on a zinc-sulphide plate kindle the precious spark? It is probably just as possible to evoke vitality out of the clash of billiard-balls as out of the clash of atoms and electrons. This allusion to billiard-balls recalls to my mind a striking passage from Tyndall's famous Belfast Address which he puts in the mouth of Bishop Butler in his imaginary argument with Lucretius, and which shows how thoroughly Tyndall appreciated the difficulties of his own position in advocating the theory of the physico-chemical origin of life.

The atomic and electronic theory of matter admits one to a world that does indeed seem unreal and fantastic. "If my bark sinks," says the poet, "'t is to another sea." If the mind breaks through what we call gross matter, and explores its interior, it finds itself indeed in a vast under or hidden world - a world almost as much a creation of the imagination as that visited by Alice in Wonderland, except that the existence of this world is capable of demonstration. It is a world of the infinitely little which science interprets in terms of the infinitely large. Sir Oliver Lodge sees the molecular spaces that separate the particles of any material body relatively like the interstellar spaces that separate the heavenly bodies. Just as all the so-called solid matter revealed by our astronomy is almost infinitesimal compared with the space through which it is distributed, so the electrons which compose the matter with which we deal are comparable to the bodies of the solar system moving in vast spaces. It is indeed a fantastic world where science conceives of bodies a thousand times smaller than the hydrogen atom - the smallest body known to science; where it conceives of vibrations in the ether millions of millions times a second; where we are bombarded by a shower of corpuscles from a burning candle, or a gas-jet, or a red-hot iron surface, moving at the speed of one hundred thousand miles a second! But this almost omnipotent ether has, after all, some of the limitations of the finite. It takes time to transmit the waves of light from the sun and the stars. This measurable speed, says Sir Oliver Lodge, gives the ether away, and shows its finite character.

It seems as if the theory of the ether must be true, because it fits in so well with the enigmatic, contradictory, incomprehensible character of the universe as revealed to our minds. We can affirm and deny almost anything of the ether - that it is immaterial, and yet the source of all material; that it is absolutely motionless, yet the cause of all motion; that it is the densest body in nature, and yet the most rarified; that it is everywhere, but defies detection; that it is as undiscoverable as the Infinite itself; that our physics cannot prove it, though they cannot get along without it. The ether inside a mass of iron or of lead is just as dense as the ether outside of it - which means that it is not dense at all, in our ordinary use of the term.

VI

There are physical changes in matter, there are chemical changes, and there is a third change, as unlike either of these as they are unlike each other. I refer to atomic change, as in radio-activity, which gives us lead from helium - a spontaneous change of the atoms. The energy that keeps the earth going, says Soddy, is to be sought for in the individual atoms; not in the great heaven-shaking voice of thunder, but in the still small voice of the atoms. Radio-activity is the mainspring of the universe. The only elements so far known that undergo spontaneous change are uranium and thorium. One pound of uranium contains and slowly gives out the same amount of energy that a hundred tons of coal evolves in its combustion, but only one ten-billionth part of this amount is given out every year.

Man, of course, reaps where he has not sown. How could it be otherwise? It takes energy to sow or plant energy. We are exhausting the coal, the natural gas, the petroleum of the rocks, the fertility of the soil. But we cannot exhaust the energy of the winds or the tides, or of falling water, because this energy is ever renewed by gravity and the sun. There can be no exhaustion of our natural mechanical and chemical resources, as some seem to fear.

I recently visited a noted waterfall in the South where electric power is being developed on a large scale. A great column of water makes a vertical fall of six hundred feet through a steel tube, and in the fall develops two hundred and fifty thousand horse-power. The water comes out of the tunnel at the bottom, precisely the same water that went in at the top; no change whatever has occurred in it, yet a vast amount of power has been taken out of it, or, rather, generated by its fall. Another drop of six hundred feet would develop as much more; in fact, the process may be repeated indefinitely, the same amount of power resulting each time, without effecting any change in the character of the water. The pull of gravity is the source of the power which is distributed hundreds of miles across the country as electricity. Two hundred and fifty thousand invisible, immaterial, noiseless horses are streaming along these wires with incredible speed to do the work of men and horses in widely separated parts of the country. A river of sand falling down those tubes, if its particles moved among themselves with the same freedom that those of the water do, would develop the same power. The attraction of gravitation is not supposed to be electricity, and yet here out of its pull upon the water comes this enormous voltage! The fact that such a mysterious and ubiquitous power as electricity can be developed from the action of matter without any alteration in its particles, suggests the question whether or not this something that we call life, or life-force, may not slumber in matter in the same way; but the secret of its development we have not yet learned, as we have that of electricity.

Radio-activity is uninfluenced by external conditions; hence we are thus far unable to control it. Nothing that is known will effect the transmutation of one element into another. It is spontaneous and uncontrollable. May not life be spontaneous in the same sense?

The release of the energy associated with the structure of the atoms is not available by any of our mechanical appliances. The process of radio-activity involves the expulsion of atoms of helium with a velocity three hundred times greater than that ever previously known for any material mass or particle, and this power we are incompetent to use. The atoms remain unchanged amid the heat and pressure of the laboratory of nature. Iron and oxygen and so forth remain the same in the sun as here on the earth.

Science strips gross matter of its grossness. When it is done with it, it is no longer the obstructive something we know and handle; it is reduced to pure energy - the line between it and spirit does not exist. We have found that bodies are opaque only to certain rays; the X-ray sees through this too too solid flesh. Bodies are ponderable only to our dull senses; to a finer hand than this the door or the wall might offer no obstruction; a finer eye than this might see the emanations from the living body; a finer ear might hear the clash of electrons in the air. Who can doubt, in view of what we already know, that forces and influences from out the heavens above, and from the earth beneath, that are beyond our ken, play upon us constantly?

The final mystery of life is no doubt involved in conditions and forces that are quite outside of or beyond our conscious life activities, in forces that play about us and upon and through us, that we know not of, because a knowledge of them is not necessary to our well-being. "Our eye takes in only an octave of the vibrations we call light," because no more is necessary for our action or our dealing with things. The invisible rays of the spectrum are potent, but they are beyond the ken of our senses. There are sounds or sound vibrations that we do not hear; our sense of touch cannot recognize a gossamer, or the gentler air movements.

I began with the contemplation of the beauty and terror of the thunderbolt - "God's autograph," as one of our poets (Joel Benton) said, "written upon the sky." Let me end with an allusion to another aspect of the storm that has no terror in it - the bow in the clouds: a sudden apparition, a cosmic phenomenon no less wonderful and startling than the lightning's flash. The storm with terror and threatened destruction on one side of it, and peace and promise on the other! The bow appears like a miracle, but it is a commonplace of nature; unstable as life, and beautiful as youth. The raindrops are not changed, the light is not changed, the laws of the storms are not changed; and yet, behold this wonder!

But all these strange and beautiful phenomena springing up in a world of inert matter are but faint symbols of the mystery and the miracle of the change of matter from the non-living to the living, from the elements in the clod to the same elements in the brain and heart of man.

IV

THE BAFFLING PROBLEM

I

Still the problem of living things haunts my mind and, let me warn my reader, will continue to haunt it throughout the greater part of this volume. The final truth about it refuses to be spoken. Every effort to do so but gives one new evidence of how insoluble the problem is.

In this world of change is there any other change to be compared with that in matter, from the dead to the living? - a change so great that most minds feel compelled to go outside of matter and invoke some super-material force or agent to account for it. The least of living things is so wonderful, the phenomena it exhibits are so fundamentally unlike those of inert matter, that we invent a word for it, *vitality*; and having got the word, we conceive of a vital force or principle to explain vital phenomena. Hence vitalism - a philosophy of living things, more or less current in the world from Aristotle's time down to our own. It conceives of something in nature super-mechanical and super-chemical, though inseparably bound up with these things. There is no life without material and chemical forces, but material and chemical forces do not hold the secret of life. This is vitalism as opposed to mechanism, or scientific materialism, which is the doctrine of the all-sufficiency of the physical forces operating in the inorganic world to give rise to all the phenomena of the organic world - a doctrine coming more and more in vogue with the progress of physical science. Without holding to any belief in the supernatural or the teleological, and while adhering to the idea that there has been, and can be, no break in the causal sequence in this world, may one still hold to some form of vitalism, and see in life something more than applied physics and chemistry?

Is biology to be interpreted in the same physical and chemical terms as geology? Are biophysics and geophysics one and the same? One may freely admit that there cannot be two kinds of physics, nor two kinds of chemistry - not one kind for a rock, and another kind for a tree, or a man. There are not two species of oxygen, nor two of carbon, nor two of hydrogen and nitrogen - one for living and one for dead matter. The water in the human body is precisely the same as the water that flows by in the creek or that comes down when it rains; and the sulphur and the lime and the iron and the phosphorus and the magnesium are identical, so far as chemical analysis can reveal, in the organic and the inorganic worlds. But are we not compelled to think of a kind of difference between a living and a non-living body that we cannot fit into any of the mechanical or chemical concepts that we apply to the latter? Professor Loeb, with his "Mechanistic Conception of Life"; Professor Henderson, of Harvard, with his "Fitness of the Environment"; Professor Le Dantec, of the Sorbonne in Paris, with his volume on "The Nature and Origin of Life," published a few years since; Professor Schaefer, President of the British Association, Professor Verworn of Bonn, and many others find in the laws and properties of matter itself a sufficient explanation of all the phenomena of life. They look upon the living body as only the sum of its physical and chemical activities; they do not seem to feel the need of accounting for life itself - for that something which confers vitality upon the heretofore non-vital elements. That there is new behavior, that there are new chemical compounds called organic, - tens of thousands of them not found in inorganic nature, - that there are new processes set up in aggregates of matter, - growth, assimilation, metabolism, reproduction, thought, emotion, science, civilization, - no one denies.

How are we going to get these things out of the old physics and chemistry without some new factor or agent or force? To help ourselves out here with a "vital principle," or with spirit, or a creative impulse, as Bergson does, seems to be the only course open to certain types of mind. Positive science cannot follow us in this step, because science is limited to the verifiable. The stream of forces with which it deals is continuous; it must find the physical equivalents of all the forces that go into the body in the output of the body, and it cannot admit of a life force which it cannot trace to the physical forces.

What has science done to clear up this mystery of vitality? Professor Loeb, our most eminent experimental biologist, has succeeded in fertilizing the eggs of some low forms of sea life by artificial means; and in one instance, at least, it is reported that the fatherless form grew to maturity. This is certainly an interesting fact, but takes us no nearer the solution of the mystery of vitality than the fact that certain chemical compounds may stimulate the organs of reproduction helps to clear up the mystery of generation; or the fact that certain other chemical compounds help the digestive and assimilative processes and further the metabolism of the body assists in clearing up the mystery that attaches to these things. In all such cases we have the living body to begin with. The egg of the sea-urchin and the egg of the jelly-fish are living beings that responded to certain chemical substances, so that a process is set going in their cell life that is equivalent to fertilization. It seems to me that the result of all Professor Loeb's valuable inquiries is only to give us a more intimate sense of how closely mechanical and chemical principles are associated and identified with all the phenomena of life and with all animal behavior. Given a living organism, mechanics and chemistry will then explain much of its behavior - practically all the behavior of the lower organisms, and much of that of the higher. Even when we reach man, our reactions to the environment and to circumstances play a great part in our lives; but dare we say that will, liberty of choice, ideation, do not play a part also? How much reality there is in the so-called animal will, is a problem; but that there is a foundation for our belief in the reality of the human will, I, for one, do not for a moment doubt. The discontinuity here is only apparent and not real. We meet with the same break when we try to get our mental states, our power of thought - a poem, a drama, a work of art, a great oration - out of the food we eat; but life does it, though our science is none the wiser for it. Our physical life forms a closed circle, science says, and what goes into our bodies as physical force, must come out in physical force, or as some of its equivalents. Well, one of the equivalents, transformed by some unknown chemism within us, is our psychic force, or states of consciousness. The two circles, the physical and the psychical, are not concentric, as Fiske fancied, but are linked in some mysterious way.

Professor Loeb is a master critic of the life processes; he and his compeers analyze them as they have never been analyzed before; but the solution of the great problem of life that we are awaiting does not come. A critic may resolve all of Shakespeare's plays into their historic and other elements, but that will not account for Shakespeare. Nature's synthesis furnishes occasions for our analysis. Most assuredly all psychic phenomena have a physical basis; we know the soul only through the body; but that they are all of physico-chemical origin, is another matter.

II

Biological science has hunted the secret of vitality like a detective; and it has done some famous work; but it has not yet unraveled the mystery. It knows well the part played by carbon, oxygen, and hydrogen in organic chemistry, that without water and carbon dioxide there could be no life; it knows the part played by light, air, heat, gravity, osmosis, chemical affinity, and all the hundreds or thousands of organic compounds; it knows the part played by what are called the enzymes, or ferments, in all living bodies, but it does not know the secret of these ferments; it knows the part played by colloids, or jelly-like compounds, that there is no living body without colloids, though there are colloid bodies that are not living; it knows the part played by oxidation, that without it a living body ceases to function, though everywhere all about us is oxidation without life; it knows the part played by chlorophyll in the vegetable kingdom, and yet how chlorophyll works such magic upon the sun's rays, using the solar energy to fix the carbon of carbonic acid in the air, and thereby storing this energy as it is stored in wood and coal and in much of the food we consume, is a mystery. Chemistry cannot repeat the process in its laboratories. The fungi do not possess this wonderful chlorophyllian power, and hence cannot use the sunbeam to snatch their carbon from the air; they must get it from decomposed vegetable matter; they feed, as the animals do, upon elements that have gone through the cycle of vegetable life. The secret of vegetable life, then, is in the green substance of the leaf where science is powerless to unlock it. Conjure with the elements as it may, it cannot produce the least speck of living matter. It can by synthesis produce many of the organic compounds, but only from matter that has already been through the organic cycle. It has lately produced rubber, but from other products of vegetable life.

As soon as the four principal elements, carbon, oxygen, hydrogen, and nitrogen, that make up the living body, have entered the world of living matter, their activities and possible combinations enormously increase; they enter into new relations with one another and form compounds of great variety and complexity, characterized by the instability which life requires. The organic compounds are vastly more sensitive to light and heat and air than are the same elements in the inorganic world. What has happened to them? Chemistry cannot tell us. Oxidation, which is only slow combustion, is the main source of energy in the body, as it is in the steam-engine. The storing of the solar energy, which occurs only in the vegetable, is by a process of reduction, that is, the separation of the carbon and oxygen in carbonic acid and water. The chemical reactions which liberate energy in the body are slow; in dead matter they are rapid and violent, or explosive and destructive. It is the chemistry in the leaf of the plant that diverts or draws the solar energy into the stream of life, and how it does it is a mystery.

The scientific explanations of life phenomena are all after the fact; they do not account for the fact; they start with the ready-made organism and then reduce its activities and processes to their physical equivalents. Vitality is given, and then the vital processes are fitted into mechanical and chemical concepts, or into moulds derived from inert matter - not a difficult thing to do, but no more an explanation of the mystery of vitality than a painting or a marble bust of Tyndall would be an explanation of that great scientist.

All Professor Loeb's experiments and criticisms throw light upon the life processes, or upon the factors that take part in them, but not upon the secret of the genesis of the processes themselves. Amid all the activities of his mechanical and chemical factors, there is ever present a factor which he ignores, which his analytical method cannot seize; namely, what Verworn calls "the specific energy of living substance." Without this, chemism and mechanism would work together to quite other ends. The water in the wave, and the laws that govern it, do not differ at all from the water and its laws that surround it; but unless one takes into account the force that makes the wave, an analysis of the phenomena will leave one where he began.

Professor Le Dantec leaves the subject where he took it up, with the origin of life and the life processes unaccounted for. His work is a description, and not an explanation. All our ideas about vitality, or an unknown factor in the organic world, he calls "mystic" and unscientific. A sharp line of demarcation between living and non-living bodies is not permissible. This, he says, is the anthropomorphic error which puts some mysterious quality or force in all bodies considered to be living. To Le Dantec, the difference between the quick and the dead is of the same order as the difference which exists between two chemical compounds - for example, as that which exists between alcohol and an aldehyde, a liquid that has two less atoms of hydrogen in its composition. Modify your chemistry a little, add or subtract an atom or two, more or less, of this or that gas, and dead matter thrills into life, or living matter sinks to the inert. In other words, life is the gift of chemistry, its particular essence is of the chemical order - a bold inference from the fact that there is no life without chemical reactions, no life without oxidation. Yet chemical reactions in the laboratory cannot produce life. With Le Dantec, biology, like geology and astronomy, is only applied mechanics and chemistry.

III

Such is the result of the rigidly objective study of life - the only method analytical science can pursue. The conception of vitality as a factor in itself answers to nothing that the objective study of life can disclose; such a study reveals a closed circle of physical forces, chemical and mechanical, into which no immaterial force or principle can find entrance. "The fact of being conscious," Le Dantec says with emphasis, "does not intervene in the slightest degree in directing vital movements." But common sense and everyday observation tell us that states of consciousness do influence the bodily processes - influence the circulation, the digestion, the secretions, the respiration.

An objective scientific study of a living body yields results not unlike those which we might get from an objective study of a book considered as something fabricated - its materials, its construction, its typography, its binding, the number of its chapters and pages, and so on - without giving any heed to the meaning of the book - its ideas, the human soul and personality that it embodies, the occasion that gave rise to it, indeed all its subjective and immaterial aspects. All these things, the whole significance of the volume, would elude scientific analysis. It would seem to be a manufactured article, representing only so much mechanics and chemistry. It is the same with the living body. Unless we permit ourselves to go behind the mere facts, the mere mechanics and chemistry of life phenomena, and interpret them in the light of immaterial principles, in short, unless we apply some sort of philosophy to them, the result of our analysis will be but dust in our eyes, and ashes in our mouths. Unless there is something like mind or intelligence pervading nature, some creative and transforming impulse that cannot be defined by our mechanical concepts, then, to me, the whole organic world is meaningless. If man is not more than an "accident in the history of the thermic evolution of the globe," or the result of the fortuitous juxtaposition and combination of carbonic acid gas and water and a few other elements, what shall we say? It is at least a bewildering proposition.

Could one by analyzing a hive of bees find out the secret of its organization - its unity as an aggregate of living insects? Behold its wonderful economics, its division of labor, its complex social structure, - the queen, the workers, the drones, - thousands of bees without any head or code of laws or directing agent, all acting as one individual, all living and working for the common good. There is no confusion or cross-purpose in the hive. When the time of swarming comes, they are all of one mind and the swarm comes forth. Who or what decides who shall stay and who shall go? When the honey supply fails, or if it fail prematurely, on account of a drought, the swarming instinct is inhibited, and the unhatched queens are killed in their cells. Who or what issues the regicide order? We can do no better than to call it the Spirit of the Hive, as Maeterlinck has done. It is a community of mind. What one bee knows and feels, they all know and feel at the same instant. Something like that is true of a living body; the cells are like the bees: they work together, they build up the tissues and organs, some are for one thing and some for another, each community of cells plays its own part, and they all pull together for the good of the whole. We can introduce cells and even whole organs, for example a kidney from another living body, and all goes well; and yet we cannot find the seat of the organization. Can we do any better than to call it the Spirit of the Body?

IV

Our French biologist is of the opinion that the artificial production of that marvel of marvels, the living cell, will yet take place in the laboratory. But the enlightened mind, he says, does not need such proof to be convinced that there is no essential difference between living and non-living matter.

Professor Henderson, though an expounder of the mechanistic theory of the origin of life, admits that he does not know of a biological chemist to whom the "mechanistic origin of a cell is scientifically imaginable." Like Professor Loeb, he starts with the vital; how he came by it we get no inkling; he confesses frankly that the biological chemist cannot even face the problem of the origin of life. He quotes with approval a remark of Liebig's, as reported by Lord Kelvin, that he (Liebig) could no more believe that a leaf or a flower could be formed or could grow by chemical forces "than a book on chemistry, or on botany, could grow out of dead matter." Is not this conceding to the vitalists all that they claim? The cell is the unit of life; all living bodies are but vast confraternities of cells, some billions or trillions of them in the human body; the cell builds up the tissues, the tissues build up the organs, the organs build up the body. Now if it is not thinkable that chemism could beget a cell, is it any more thinkable that it could build a living tissue, and then an organ, and then the body as a whole? If there is an inscrutable something at work at the start, which organizes that wonderful piece of vital mechanism, the cell, is it any the less operative ever after, in all life processes, in all living bodies and their functions, - the vital as distinguished from the mechanical and chemical? Given the cell, and you have only to multiply it, and organize these products into industrial communities, and direct them to specific ends, - certainly a task which we would not assign to chemistry or physics any more than we would assign to them the production of a work on chemistry or botany, - and you have all the myriad forms of terrestrial life.

The cell is the parent of every living thing on the globe; and if it is unthinkable that the material and irrational forces of inert matter could produce it, then mechanics and chemistry must play second fiddle in all that whirl and dance of the atoms that make up life. And that is all the vitalists claim. The physico-chemical forces do play second fiddle; that inexplicable something that we call vitality dominates and leads them. True it is that a living organism yields to scientific analysis only mechanical and chemical forces - a fact which only limits the range of scientific analysis, and which by no means exhausts the possibilities of the living organism. The properties of matter and the laws of matter are intimately related to life, yea, are inseparable from it, but they are by no means the whole story. Professor Henderson repudiates the idea of any extra-physical influence as being involved in the processes of life, and yet concedes that the very foundation of all living matter, yea, the whole living universe in embryo - the cell - is beyond the possibilities of physics and chemistry alone. Mechanism and chemism are adequate to account for astronomy and geology, and therefore, he thinks, are sufficient to account for biology, without calling in the aid of any Bergsonian life impulse. Still these forces stand impotent before that microscopic world, the cell, the foundation of all life.

Our professor makes the provisional statement, not in obedience to his science, but in obedience to his philosophy, that something more than mechanics and chemistry may have had a hand in shaping the universe, some primordial tendency impressed upon or working in matter "just before mechanism begins to act" - "a necessary and preestablished associate of mechanism." So that if we start with the universe, with life, and with this tendency, mechanism will do all the rest. But this is not science, of course, because it is not verifiable; it is practically the philosophy of Bergson.

The cast-iron conclusions of physical science do pinch the Harvard professor a bit, and he pads them with a little of the Bergsonian philosophy. Bergson himself is not pinched at all by the conclusions of positive science. He sees that we, as human beings, cannot live in this universe without supplementing our science with some sort of philosophy that will help us to escape from the fatalism of matter and force into the freedom of the spiritual life. If we are merely mechanical and chemical accidents, all the glory of life, all the meaning of our moral and spiritual natures, go by the board.

Professor Henderson shows us how well this planet, with its oceans and continents, and its mechanical and chemical forces and elements, is suited to sustain life, but he brings us no nearer the solution of the mystery than we were before. His title, to begin with, is rather bewildering. Has the "fitness of the environment" ever been questioned? The environment is fit, of course, else living bodies would not be here. We are used to taking hold of the other end of the problem. In living nature the foot is made to fit the shoe, and not the shoe the foot. The environment is the mould in which the living organism is cast. Hence, it seems to me, that seeking to prove the fitness of the environment is very much like seeking to prove the fitness of water for fish to swim in, or the fitness of the air for birds to fly in. The implication seems to be made that the environment anticipates the organism, or meets it half way. But the environment is rather uncompromising. Man alone modifies his environment by the weapon of science; but not radically; in the end he has to fit himself to it. Life has been able to adjust itself to the universal forces and so go along with them; otherwise we should not be here. We may say, humanly speaking, that the water is friendly to the swimmer, if he knows how to use it; if not, it is his deadly enemy. The same is true of all the elements and forces of nature. Whether they be for or against us, depends upon ourselves. The wind is never tempered to the shorn lamb, the shorn lamb must clothe itself against the wind. Life is adaptive, and this faculty of adaptation to the environment, of itself takes it out of the category of the physico-chemical. The rivers and seas favor navigation, if we have gumption enough to use and master their forces. The air is good to breathe, and food to eat, for those creatures that are adapted to them. Bergson thinks, not without reason, that life on other planets may be quite different from what it is on our own, owing to a difference in chemical and physical conditions. Change the chemical constituents of sea water, and you radically change the lower organisms. With an atmosphere entirely of oxygen, the processes of life would go on more rapidly and perhaps reach a higher form of development. Life on this planet is limited to a certain rather narrow range of temperature; the span may be the same in other worlds, but farther up or farther down the scale. Had the air been differently constituted, would not our lungs have been different? The lungs of the fish are in his gills: he has to filter his air from a much heavier medium. The nose of the pig is fitted for rooting; shall we say, then, that the soil was made friable that pigs might root in it? The webbed foot is fitted to the water; shall we say, then, that water is liquid in order that geese and ducks may swim in it? One more atom of oxygen united to the two atoms that go to make the molecule of air, and we should have had ozone instead of the air we now breathe. How unsuited this would have made the air for life as we know it! Oxidation would have consumed us rapidly. Life would have met this extra atom by some new device.

One wishes Professor Henderson had told us more about how life fits itself to the environment - how matter, moved and moulded only by mechanical and chemical forces, yet has some power of choice that a machine does not have, and can and does select the environment best suited to its well-being. In fact, that it should have, or be capable of, any condition of well-being, if it is only a complex of physical and chemical forces, is a problem to wrestle with. The ground we walk on is such a complex, but only the living bodies it supports have conditions of well-being.

Professor Henderson concedes very little to the vitalists or the teleologists. He is a thorough mechanist. "Matter and energy," he says, "have an original property, assuredly not by chance, which organizes the universe in space and time." Where or how matter got this organizing property, he offers no opinion. "Given the universe, life, and the tendency [the tendency to organize], mechanism is inductively proved sufficient to

John Burroughs

account for all phenomena." Biology, then, is only mechanics and chemistry engaged in a new role without any change of character; but what put them up to this new role? "The whole evolutionary process, both cosmic and organic, is one, and the biologist may now rightly regard the universe in its very essence as biocentric."

V

Another Harvard voice is less pronounced in favor of the mechanistic conception of life. Professor Rand thinks that in a mechanically determined universe, "our conscious life becomes a meaningless replica of an inexorable physical concatenation" - the soul the result of a fortuitous concourse of atoms. Hence all the science and art and literature and religion of the world are merely the result of a molecular accident.

Dr. Rand himself, in wrestling with the problem of organization in a late number of "Science," seems to hesitate whether or not to regard man as a molecular accident, an appearance presented to us by the results of the curious accidents of molecules - which is essentially Professor Loeb's view; or whether to look upon the living body as the result of a "specific something" that organizes, that is, of "dominating organic agencies," be they psychic or super-mundane, which dominate and determine the organization of the different parts of the body into a whole. Yet he is troubled with the idea that this specific something may be "nothing more than accidental chemical peculiarities of cells." But would these accidental peculiarities be constant? Do accidents happen millions of times in the same way? The cell is without variableness or shadow of turning. The cells are the minute people that build up all living forms, and what prompts them to build a man in the one case, and the man's dog in another, is the mystery that puzzles Professor Rand. "Tissue cells," he says, "are not structures like stone blocks laboriously carved and immovably cemented in place. They are rather like the local eddies in an ever-flowing and ever-changing stream of fluids. Substance which was at one moment a part of a cell, passes out and a new substance enters. What is it that prevents the local whirl in this unstable stream from changing its form? How is it that a million muscle cells remain alike, collectively ready to respond to a nerve impulse?" According to one view, expressed by Professor Rand, "Organization is something that we read into natural phenomena. It is in itself nothing." The alternative view holds that there is a specific organizing agent that brings about the harmonious operation of all the organs and parts of the system - a superior dynamic force controlling and guiding all the individual parts.

A most determined and thorough-going attempt to hunt down the secret of vitality, and to determine how far its phenomena can be interpreted in terms of mechanics and chemistry, is to be found in Professor H. W. Conn's volume entitled "The Living Machine." Professor Conn justifies his title by defining a machine as "a piece of apparatus so designed that it can change one kind of energy into another for a definite purpose." Of course the adjective "living" takes it out of the category of all mere mechanical devices and makes it super-mechanical, just as Haeckel's application of the word "living" to his inorganics ("living inorganics"), takes them out of the category of the inorganic. In every machine, properly so called, all the factors are known; but do we know all the factors in a living body? Professor Conn applies his searching analysis to most of the functions of the human body, to digestion, to assimilation, to circulation, to respiration, to metabolism, and so on, and he finds in every function something that does not fall within his category - some force not mechanical nor chemical, which he names vital.

In following the processes of digestion, all goes well with his chemistry and his mechanics till he comes to the absorption of food-particles, or their passage through the walls of the intestines into the blood. Here, the ordinary physical forces fail him, and living matter comes to his aid. The inner wall of the intestine is not a lifeless membrane, and osmosis will not solve the mystery. There is something there that seizes hold of the droplets of oil by means of little extruded processes, and then passes them through its own body to excrete them on an inner surface into the blood-vessels. "This fat absorption thus appears to be a vital process and not one simply controlled by physical forces like osmosis. Here our explanation runs against what we call 'vital power' of the ultimate elements of the body." Professor Conn next analyzes the processes of circulation, and his ready-made mechanical concepts carry him along swimmingly, till he tries to explain by them the beating of the heart, and the contraction of the small blood-vessels which regulate the blood-supply. Here comes in play the mysterious vital power again. He comes upon the same power when he tries to determine what it is that enables the muscle-fibre to take from the lymph the material needed for its use, and to discard the rest. The fibre acts as if it knew what it wanted - a very unmechanical attribute.

Then Professor Conn applies his mechanics and chemistry to the respiratory process and, of course, makes out a very clear case till he comes to the removal of the waste, or ash. The steam-engine cannot remove its own ash; the "living machine" can. Much of this ash takes the form of urea, and "the seizing upon the urea by the kidney cells is a vital phenomenon." Is not the peristaltic movement of the bowels, by which the solid matter is removed, also a vital phenomenon? Is not the conception of a pipe or a tube that forces semi-fluid matter along its hollow interior, by the contraction of its walls, quite beyond the reach of mechanics? The force is as mechanical as the squeezing of the bulb of a syringe by the hand, but in the case of the intestines, what does the squeezing? The vital force?

When the mechanical and chemical concepts are applied to the phenomena of the nervous system, they work very well till we come to mental phenomena. When we try to correlate physical energy with thought or consciousness, we are at the end of our tether. Here is a gulf we cannot span. The theory of the machine breaks down. Some other force than material force is demanded here, namely, psychical, - a force or principle quite beyond the sphere of the analytic method.

Hence Professor Conn concludes that there are vital factors and that they are the primal factors in the organism. The mechanical and chemical forces are the secondary factors. It is the primal factors that elude scientific analysis. Why a muscle contracts, or why a gland secretes, or "why the oxidation of starch in the living machine gives rise to motion, growth, and reproduction, while if the oxidation occurs in the chemist's laboratory ... it simply gives rise to heat," are questions he cannot answer. In all his inquiries into the parts played by mechanical and chemical laws in the organism, he is compelled to "assume as their foundation the simple vital properties of living phenomena."

VI

It should not surprise nor disturb us that the scientific interpretation of life leads to materialism, or to the conviction of the all-sufficiency of the mechanical and chemical forces of dead matter to account for all living phenomena. It need not surprise us because positive science, as such, can deal only with physical and chemical forces. If there is anything in this universe besides physical and chemical force, science does not know it. It does not know it because it is absolutely beyond the reach of its analysis. When we go beyond the sphere of the concrete, the experimental, the verifiable, only our philosophy can help us. The world within us, the world of psychic forces, is beyond the ken of science. It can analyze the living body, trace all its vital processes, resolve them into their mechanical and chemical equivalents, show us the parts played by the primary elements, the part played by the enzymes, or ferments, and the like, and yet it cannot tell us the secret of life - of that which makes organic chemistry so vastly different from inorganic. It discloses to us the wonders of the cell - a world of mystery by itself; it analyzes the animal body into organs, and the organs into tissues, and the tissues into cells, but the secret of organization utterly baffles it. After Professor Wilson had concluded his masterly work on the cell, he was forced to admit that the final mystery of the cell eluded him, and that his investigation "on the whole seemed to widen rather than to narrow the enormous gap that separates even the lowest forms of life from the inorganic world."

All there is outside the sphere of physical science belongs to religion, to philosophy, to art, to literature. Huxley spoke strictly and honestly as a man of science, when he related consciousness to the body, as the sound of a clock when it strikes is related to the machinery of the clock. The scientific analysis of a living body reveals nothing but the action of the mechanical and chemical principles. If you analyze it by fire or by cremation, you get gases and vapors and mineral ash, that is all; the main thing about the live body - its organization, its life - you do not get. Of course science knows this; and to account for this missing something, it philosophizes, and relegates it to the interior world of molecular physics - it is all in the way the ultimate particles of matter were joined or compounded, were held together in the bonds of molecular matrimony. What factor or agent or intelligence is active or directive in this molecular marriage of the atoms, science does not inquire. Only philosophy can deal with that problem.

What can science see or find in the brain of man that answers to the soul? Only certain movements of matter in the brain cortex. What difference does it find between inert matter and a living organism? Only a vastly more complex mechanics and chemistry in the latter. A wide difference, not of kind, but of degree. The something we call vitality, that a child recognizes, science does not find; vitality is something *sui generis*. Scientific analysis cannot show us the difference between the germ cell of a starfish and the germ cell of a man; and yet think of what a world of difference is hidden in those microscopic germs! What force is there in inert matter that can build a machine by the adjustment of parts to each other? We can explain the most complex chemical compounds by the action of chemical forces and chemical affinity, but they cannot explain that adjustment of parts to each other, the cooerdination of their activities that makes a living machine.

In organized matter there is something that organizes. "The cell itself is an organization of smaller units," and to drive or follow the organizing principle into the last hiding-place is past the power of biological chemistry. What constitutes the guiding force or principle of a living body, adjusting all its parts, making them pull together, making of the circulation one system in which the heart, the veins, the arteries, the lungs, all work to one common end, cooerdinating several different organs into a digestive system, and other parts into the nervous system, is a mystery that no objective analysis of the body can disclose.

To refer vitality to complexity alone, is to dodge the question.

Multiplying the complexity of a machine, say of a watch, any conceivable number of times would not make it any the less a machine, or change it from the automatic order to the vital order. A motor-car is a vastly more complex mechanism than a wheelbarrow, and yet it is not the less a machine. On the other hand, an amoeba is a far simpler animal than a man, and yet it is just as truly living. To refer life to complexity does not help us; we want to know what lies back of the complexity - what makes it a new species of complexity.

We cannot explain the origin of living matter by the properties which living matter possesses. There are three things that mechanics and chemistry cannot explain: the relation of the psychical to the physical through the law of the conservation and correlation of forces; the agent or principle that guides the blind chemical and physical forces so as to produce the living body; and the kind of forces that have contributed to the origin of that morphological unit - the cell.

A Western university professor in a recent essay sounds quite a different note on this subject from the one that comes to us from Harvard. Says Professor Otto C. Glaser, of the University of Michigan, in a recent issue of the "Popular Science Monthly": "Does not the fitness of living things; the fact that they perform acts useful to themselves in an environment which is constantly shifting, and often very harsh; the fact that in general everything during development, during digestion, during any of the complicated chains of processes which we find, happens at the right time, in the right place, and to the proper extent; does not all this force us to believe that there is involved something more than mere chemistry and physics? - something, not consciousness necessarily, yet its analogue - a vital x?"

There is this suggestive fact about these recent biological experiments of Dr. Carrel, of the Rockefeller Institute: they seem to prove that the life of a man is not merely the sum of the life of the myriad cells of his body. Stab the man to death, and the cells of his body still live and will continue to live if grafted upon another live man. Probably every part of the body would continue to live and grow indefinitely, in the proper medium. That the cell life should continue after the soul life has ceased is very significant. It seems a legitimate inference from this fact that the human body is the organ or instrument of some agent that is not of the body. The functional or physiological life of the body as a whole, also seems quite independent of our conscious volitional or psychic life. That which repairs and renews the body, heals its wounds, controls and coordinates its parts, adapts it to its environment, carries on its processes during sleep, in fact in all our involuntary life, seems quite independent of the man himself. Is the spirit of a race or a nation, or of the times in which we live, another illustration of the same mysterious entity?

If the vital principle, or vital force, is a fiction, invented to give the mind something to take hold of, we are in no worse case than we are in some other matters. Science tells us that there is no such *thing* as heat, or light; these are only modes of activity in matter.

In the same way we seem forced to think of life, vitality, as an entity - a fact as real as electricity or light, though it may be only a mode of motion. It may be of physico-chemical origin, as much so as heat, or light; and yet it is something as distinctive as they are among material things, and is involved in the same mystery. Is magnetism or gravitation a real thing? or, in the moral world, is love, charity, or consciousness itself? The world seems to be run by nonentities. Heat, light, life, seem nonentities. That which organizes the different parts or organs of the human body into a unit, and makes of the many organs one organism, is a nonentity. That which makes an oak an oak, and a pine a pine, is a nonentity. That which makes a sheep a sheep, and an ox an ox, is to science a nonentity. To physical science the soul is a nonentity.

There is something in the cells of the muscles that makes them contract, and in the cells of the heart that makes it beat; that something is not active in the other cells of the body. But it is a nonentity. The body is a machine and a laboratory combined, but that which cooerdinates them and makes them work together - what is that? Another nonentity. That which distinguishes a living machine from a dead machine, science has no name for, except molecular attraction and repulsion, and these are names merely; they are nonentities. Is there not molecular attraction and repulsion in a steam-engine also? And yet it is not alive. What has to supplement the mechanical and the chemical to make matter alive? We have no name for it but the vital, be it an entity or a nonentity. We have no name for a flash of lightning but electricity, be it an entity or a nonentity. We have no name for that which distinguishes a man from a brute, but mind, soul, be it an entity or a nonentity. We have no name for that which distinguishes the organic from the inorganic but vitality, be it an entity or a nonentity.

VII

Without metaphysics we can do nothing; without mental concepts, where are we? Natural selection is as much a metaphysical phrase as is consciousness, or the subjective and the objective. Natural selection is not an entity, it is a name for what we conceive of as a process. It is natural rejection as well. The vital principle is a metaphysical concept; so is instinct; so is reason; so is the soul; so is God.

Many of our concepts have been wrong. The concept of witches, of disease as the work of evil spirits, of famine and pestilence as the visitation of the wrath of God, and the like, were unfounded. Science sets us right about all such matters. It corrects our philosophy, but it cannot dispense with the philosophical attitude of mind. The philosophical must supplement the experimental.

In fact, in considering this question of life, it is about as difficult for the unscientific mind to get along without postulating a vital principle or force - which, Huxley says, is analogous to the idea of a principle of aquosity in water - as it is to walk upon the air, or to hang one's coat upon a sunbeam. It seems as if something must breathe upon the dead matter, as at the first, to make it live. Yet if there is a distinct vital force it must be correlated with physical force, it must be related causally to the rest. The idea of a vital force as something new and distinct and injected into matter from without at a given time and place in the earth's history, must undoubtedly be given up. Instead of escaping from mechanism, this notion surrenders one into the hands of mechanism, since to supplement or reinforce a principle with some other principle from without, is strictly a mechanical procedure. But the conception of vitality as potential in matter, or of the whole universe as permeated with spirit, which to me is the same thing, is a conception that takes life out of the categories of the fortuitous and the automatic.

No doubt but that all things in the material world are causally related, no doubt of the constancy of matter and force, no doubt but that all phenomena are the result of natural principles, no doubt that the living arose from the non-living, no doubt that the evolution process was inherent in the constitution of the world; and yet there is a mystery about it all that is insoluble. The miracle of vitality takes place behind a veil that we cannot penetrate, in the inmost sanctuary of the molecules of matter, in that invisible, imaginary world on the borderland between the material and the immaterial. We may fancy that it is here that the psychical effects its entrance into the physical - that spirit weds matter - that the creative energy kindles the spark we call vitality. At any rate, vitality evidently begins in that inner world of atoms and molecules; but whether as the result of their peculiar and very complex compounding or as the cause of the compounding - how are we ever to know? Is it not just as scientific to postulate a new principle, the principle of vitality, as to postulate a new process, or a new behavior of an old principle? In either case, we are in the world of the unverifiable; we take a step in the dark. Most of us, I fancy, will sympathize with George Eliot, who says in one of her letters: "To me the Development Theory, and all other explanations of processes by which things came to be, produce a feeble impression compared with the mystery that lies under the processes."

V

SCIENTIFIC VITALISM

I

All living bodies, when life leaves them, go back to the earth
from whence they came. What was it in the first instance that
gathered their elements from the earth and built them up into
such wonderful mechanisms? If we say it was nature, do we
mean by nature a physical force or an immaterial principle?
Did the earth itself bring forth a man, or did something
breathe upon the inert clay till it became a living spirit?

As life is a physical phenomenon, appearing in a concrete
physical world, it is, to that extent, within the domain of
physical science, and appeals to the scientific mind. Physical
science is at home only in the experimental, the verifiable. Its
domain ends where that of philosophy begins.

The question of how life arose in a universe of dead matter is
just as baffling a question to the ordinary mind, as how the
universe itself arose. If we assume that the germs of life drifted
to us from other spheres, propelled by the rays of the sun, or
some other celestial agency, as certain modern scientific
philosophers have assumed, we have only removed the mystery
farther away from us. If we assume that it came by
spontaneous generation, as Haeckel and others assume, then
we are only cutting a knot which we cannot untie. The god of

spontaneous generation is as miraculous as any other god. We cannot break the causal sequence without a miracle. If something came from nothing, then there is not only the end of the problem, but also the end of our boasted science.

Science is at home in discussing all the material manifestations of life - the parts played by colloids and ferments, by fluids and gases, and all the organic compounds, and by mechanical and chemical principles; it may analyze and tabulate all life processes, and show the living body as a most wonderful and complex piece of mechanism, but before the question of the origin of life itself it stands dumb, and, when speaking through such a man as Tyndall, it also stands humble and reverent. After Tyndall had, to his own satisfaction, reduced all like phenomena to mechanical attraction and repulsion, he stood with uncovered head before what he called the "mystery and miracle of vitality." The mystery and miracle lie in the fact that in the organic world the same elements combine with results so different from those of the inorganic world. Something seems to have inspired them with a new purpose. In the inorganic world, the primary elements go their ceaseless round from compound to compound, from solid to fluid or gaseous, and back again, forming the world of inert matter as we know it, but in the organic world the same elements form thousands of new combinations unknown to them before, and thus give rise to the myriad forms of life that inhabit the earth.

The much-debated life question has lately found an interesting exponent in Professor Benjamin Moore, of the University of Liverpool. His volume on the subject in the "Home University Library" is very readable, and, in many respects, convincing. At least, so far as it is the word of exact science on the subject it is convincing; so far as it is speculative, or philosophical, it is or is not convincing, according to the type of mind of the reader. Professor Moore is not a bald mechanist or materialist like Professor Loeb, or Ernst Haeckel, nor is he an idealist or spiritualist, like Henri Bergson or Sir Oliver Lodge. He may be called a scientific vitalist. He keeps close to lines of scientific research as these lines lead him through the maze of the primordial elements of matter, from electron to atom, from atom to molecule, from molecule to colloid, and so up to the border of the living world. His analysis of the processes of molecular physics as they appear in the organism leads him to recognize and to name a new force, or a new manifestation of force, which he hesitates to call vital, because of the associations of this term with a prescientific age, but which he calls "biotic energy."

Biotic energy is peculiar to living bodies, and "there are precisely the same criteria for its existence," says Professor Moore, "as for the existence of any one of the inorganic energy types, viz., a set of discrete phenomena; and its nature is as mysterious to us as the cause of any one of these inorganic forms about which also we know so little. It is biotic energy which guides the development of the ovum, which regulates the exchanges of the cell, and causes such phenomena as nerve impulse, muscular contraction, and gland secretion, and it is a form of energy which arises in colloidal structures, just as magnetism appears in iron, or radio-activity in uranium or radium, and in its manifestations it undergoes exchanges with other forms of energy, in the same manner as these do among one another."

Like Professor Henderson, Professor Moore concedes to the vitalists about all they claim - namely, that there is some form of force or manifestation of energy peculiar to living bodies, and one that cannot be adequately described in terms of physics and chemistry. Professor Moore says this biotic energy "arises in colloidal structures," and so far as biochemistry can make out, arises *spontaneously* and gives rise to that marvelous bit of mechanism, the cell. In the cell appears "a form of energy unknown outside life processes which leads the mazy dance of life from point to point, each new development furnishing a starting point for the next one." It not only leads the dance along our own line of descent from our remote ancestors - it leads the dance along the long road of evolution from the first unicellular form in the dim palaeozoic seas to the complex and highly specialized forms of our own day.

The secret of this life force, or biotic energy, according to Professor Moore, is in the keeping of matter itself. The steps or stages from the depths of matter by which life arose, lead up from that imaginary something, the electron, to the inorganic colloids, or to the crystallo-colloids, which are the threshold of life, each stage showing some new transformation of energy. There must be an all-potent energy transformation before we can get chemical energy out of physical energy, and then biotic energy out of chemical energy. This transformation of inorganic energy into life energy cannot be traced or repeated in the laboratory, yet science believes the secret will sometime be in its hands. It is here that the materialistic philosophers, such as Professors Moore and Loeb, differ from the spiritualistic philosophers, such as Bergson, Sir Oliver Lodge, Professor Thompson, and others.

Professor Moore has no sympathy with those narrow mechanistic views that see in the life processes "no problems save those of chemistry and physics." "Each link in the living chain may be physico-chemical, but the chain as a whole, and its purpose, is something else." He draws an analogy from the production of music in which purely physical factors are concerned; the laws of harmonics account for all; but back of all is something that is not mechanical and chemical - there is the mind of the composer, and the performers, and the auditors, and something that takes cognizance of the whole effect. A complete human philosophy cannot be built upon physical science alone. He thinks the evolution of life from inert matter is of the same type as the evolution of one form of matter from another, or the evolution of one form of energy from another - a mystery, to be sure, but little more startling in the one case than in the other. "The fundamental mystery lies in the existence of those entities, or things, which we call matter and energy," out of the play and interaction of which all life phenomena have arisen. Organic evolution is a series of energy exchanges and transformations from lower to higher, but science is powerless to go behind the phenomena presented and name or verify the underlying mystery. Only philosophy can do this. And Professor Moore turns philosopher when he says there is beauty and design in it all, "and an eternal purpose which is ever progressing."

Bergson sets forth his views of evolution in terms of literature and philosophy. Professor Moore embodies similar views in his volume, set forth in terms of molecular science. Both make evolution a creative and a continuous process. Bergson lays the emphasis upon the cosmic spirit interacting with matter. Professor Moore lays the emphasis upon the indwelling potencies of matter itself (probably the same spirit conceived of in different terms). Professor Moore philosophizes as truly as does Bergson when he says "there must exist a whole world of living creatures which the microscope has never shown us, leading up to the bacteria and the protozoa. The brink of life lies not at the production of protozoa and bacteria, which are highly developed inhabitants of our world, but away down among the colloids; and the beginning of life was not a fortuitous event occurring millions of years ago and never again repeated, but one which in its primordial stages keeps on repeating itself all the time in our generation. So that if all intelligent creatures were by some holocaust destroyed, up out of the depths in process of millions of years, intelligent beings would once more emerge." This passage shows what a speculative leap or flight the scientific mind is at times compelled to take when it ventures beyond the bounds of positive methods. It is good philosophy, I hope, but we cannot call it science. Thrilled with cosmic emotion, Walt Whitman made a similar daring assertion: -

"There is no stoppage, and never can be stoppage, If I, you, and the worlds, and all beneath or upon their surfaces, were this moment reduced back to a pallid float, it would not avail in the long run, We should surely bring up again where we now stand, And surely go as much farther, and then farther and farther."

II

Evolution is creative, whether it works in matter - as Bergson describes, or whether its path lies up through electrons and atoms and molecules, as Professor Moore describes. There is something that creates and makes matter plastic to its will. Whether we call matter "the living garment of God," as Goethe did, or a reservoir of creative energy, as Tyndall and his school did, and as Professor Moore still does, we are paying homage to a power that is super-material. Life came to our earth, says Professor Moore, through a "well-regulated orderly development," and it "comes to every mother earth of the universe in the maturity of her creation when the conditions arrive within suitable limits." That no intelligent beings appeared upon the earth for millions upon millions of years, that for whole geologic ages there was no creature with more brains than a snail possesses, shows the almost infinitely slow progress of development, and that there has been no arbitrary or high-handed exercise of creative power. The universe is not run on principles of modern business efficiency, and man is at the head of living forms, not by the fiat of some omnipotent power, some superman, but as the result of the operation of forces that balk at no delay, or waste, or failure, and that are dependent upon the infinitely slow ripening and amelioration of both cosmic and terrestrial conditions.

We do not get rid of God by any such dictum, but we get rid of the anthropomorphic views which we have so long been wont to read into the processes of nature. We dehumanize the universe, but we do not render it the less grand and mysterious. Professor Moore points out to us how life came to a cooling planet as soon as the temperature became low enough for certain chemical combinations to appear. There must first be oxides and saline compounds, there must be carbonates of calcium and magnesium, and the like. As the temperature falls, more and more complex compounds, such as life requires, appear; till, in due time, carbon dioxide and water are at hand, and life can make a start. At the white heat of some of the fixed stars, the primary chemical elements are not yet evolved; but more and more elements appear, and more and more complex compounds are formed as the cooling process progresses.

"This note cannot be too strongly sounded, that as matter is allowed capacity for assuming complex forms, those complex forms appear. As soon as oxides can be there, oxides appear; when temperature admits of carbonates, then carbonates are forthwith formed. These are experiments which any chemist can to-day repeat in a crucible. And on a cooling planet, as soon as temperature will admit the presence of life, then life appears, as the evidence of geology shows us." When we speak of the beginning of life, it is not clear just what we mean. The unit of all organized bodies is the cell, but the cell is itself an organized body, and must have organic matter to feed upon. Hence the cell is only a more complex form of more primitive living matter. As we go down the scale toward the inorganic, can we find the point where the living and the non-living meet and become one? "Life had to surge a long way up from the depths before a green plant cell came into being." When the green plant cell was found, life was fairly launched. This plant cell, in the form of chlorophyll, by the aid of water and the trace of carbon dioxide in the air, began to store up the solar energy in fruit and grain and woody tissue, and thus furnish power to run all forms of life machinery.

The materialists or naturalists are right in urging that we live in a much more wonderful universe than we have ever imagined, and that in matter itself sleep potencies and possibilities not dreamt of in our philosophy. The world of complex though invisible activities which science reveals all about us, the solar and stellar energies raining upon us from above, the terrestrial energies and influences playing through us from below, the transformations and transmutations taking place on every hand, the terrible alertness and potency of the world of inert matter as revealed by a flash of lightning, the mysteries of chemical affinity, of magnetism, of radio-activity, all point to deep beneath deep in matter itself. It is little wonder that men who dwell habitually upon these things and are saturated with the spirit and traditions of laboratory investigation, should believe that in some way matter itself holds the mystery of the origin of life. On the other hand, a different type of mind, the more imaginative, artistic, and religious type, recoils from the materialistic view.

The sun is the source of all terrestrial energy, but the different forms that energy takes - in the plant, in the animal, in the brain of man - this type of mind is bound to ask questions about that. Gravity pulls matter down; life lifts it up; chemical forces pull it to pieces; vital forces draw it together and organize it; the winds and the waters dissolve and scatter it; vegetation recaptures and integrates it and gives it new qualities. At every turn, minds like that of Sir Oliver Lodge are compelled to think of life as a principle or force doing something with matter. The physico-chemical forces will not do in the hands of man what they do in the hands of Nature. Such minds, therefore, feel justified in thinking that something which we call "the hands of Nature," plays a part - some principle or force which the hands of man do not hold.

John Burroughs

VI

A BIRD OF PASSAGE

I

There is one phase of the much-discussed question of the nature and origin of life which, so far as I know, has not been considered either by those who hold a brief for the physico-chemical view or by those who stand for some form of vitalism or idealism. I refer to the small part that life plays in the total scheme of things. The great cosmic machine would go on just as well without it. Its relation to the whole appears to be little different from that of a man to the train in which he journeys. Life rides on the mechanical and chemical forces, but it does not seem to be a part of them, nor identical with them, because they were before it, and will continue after it is gone.

The everlasting, all-inclusive thing in this universe seems to be inert matter with the energy it holds; while the slight, flitting, casual thing seems to be living matter. The inorganic is from all eternity to all eternity; it is distributed throughout all space and endures through all time, while the organic is, in comparison, only of the here and the now; it was not here yesterday, and it may not be here to-morrow; it comes and goes. Life is like a bird of passage which alights and tarries for a time and is gone, and the places where it perched and nested and led forth its brood know it no more. Apparently it flits from world to world as the great cosmic spring comes to each, and departs as the cosmic winter returns to each. It is a visitor, a migrant, a frail, timid thing, which waits upon the seasons and flees from the coming tempests and vicissitudes.

How casual, uncertain, and inconsequential the vital order seems in our own solar system - a mere incident or by-product in its cosmic evolution! Astronomy sounds the depths of space, and sees only mechanical and chemical forces at work there. It is almost certain that only a small fraction of the planetary surfaces is the abode of life. On the earth alone, of all the great family of planets and satellites, is the vital order in full career. It may yet linger upon Mars, but it is evidently waning. On the inferior planets it probably had its day long ago, while it must be millions of years before it comes to the superior planets, if it ever comes to them. What a vast, inconceivable outlay of time and energy for such small returns! Evidently the vital order is only an episode, a transient or secondary phase of matter in the process of sidereal evolution. Astronomic space is strewn with dead worlds, as a New England field is with drift boulders. That life has touched and tarried here and there upon them can hardly be doubted, but if it is anything more than a passing incident, an infant crying in the night, a flush of color upon the cheek, a flower blooming by the wayside, appearances are against it.

We read our astronomy and geology in the light of our enormous egotism, and appropriate all to ourselves; but science sees in our appearance here a no more significant event than in the foam and bubbles that whirl and dance for a moment upon the river's current. The bubbles have their reason for being; all the mysteries of molecular attraction and repulsion may be involved in their production; without the solar energy, and the revolution of the earth upon its axis, they would not appear; and yet they are only bubbles upon the river's current, as we are bubbles upon the stream of energy that flows through the universe. Apparently the cosmic game is played for us no more than for the parasites that infest our bodies, or for the frost ferns that form upon our window-panes in winter. The making of suns and systems goes on in the depths of space, and doubtless will go on to all eternity, without any more reference to the vital order than to the chemical compounds.

The amount of living matter in the universe, so far as we can penetrate it, compared with the non-living, is, in amount, like a flurry of snow that whitens the fields and hills of a spring morning compared to the miles of rock and soil beneath it; and with reference to geologic time it is about as fleeting. In the vast welter of suns and systems in the heavens above us, we see only dead matter, and most of it is in a condition of glowing metallic vapor. There are doubtless living organisms upon some of the invisible planetary bodies, but they are probably as fugitive and temporary as upon our own world. Much of the surface of the earth is clothed in a light vestment of life, which, back in geologic time, seems to have more completely enveloped it than at present, as both the arctic and the antarctic regions bear evidence in their coal-beds and other fossil remains of luxuriant vegetable growths.

Strip the earth of its thin pellicle of soil, thinner with reference to the mass than is the peel to the apple, and you have stripped it of its life. Or, rob it of its watery vapor and the carbon dioxide in the air, both stages in its evolution, and you have a dead world. The huge globe swings through space only as a mass of insensate rock. So limited and evanescent is the world of living matter, so vast and enduring is the world of the non-living. Looked at in this way, in the light of physical science, life, I repeat, seems like a mere passing phase of the cosmic evolution, a flitting and temporary stage of matter which it passes through in the procession of changes on the surface of a cooling planet. Between the fiery mist of the nebula, and the frigid and consolidated globe, there is a brief span, ranging over about one hundred and twenty degrees of temperature, where life appears and organic evolution takes place. Compared with the whole scale of temperature, from absolute zero to the white heat of the hottest stars, it is about a hand's-breadth compared to a mile.

Life processes cease, but chemical and mechanical processes go on forever. Life is as fugitive and uncertain as the bow in the clouds, and, like the bow in the clouds, is confined to a limited range of conditions. Like the bow, also, it is a perpetual creation, a constant becoming, and its source is not in the matter through which it is manifested, though inseparable from it. The material substance of life, like the rain-drops, is in perpetual flux and change; it hangs always on the verge of dissolution and vanishes when the material conditions fail, to be renewed again when they return. We know, do we not? that life is as literally dependent upon the sun as is the rainbow, and equally dependent upon the material elements; but whether the physical conditions sum up the whole truth about it, as they do with the bow, is the insoluble question. Science says "Yes," but our philosophy and our religion say "No." The poets and the prophets say "No," and our hopes and aspirations say "No."

II

Where, then, shall we look for the key to this mysterious thing we call life? Modern biochemistry will not listen to the old notion of a vital force - that is only a metaphysical will-o'-the-wisp that leaves us floundering in the quagmire. If I question the forces about me, what answer do I get? Molecular attraction and repulsion seem to say, "It is not in us; we are as active in the clod as in the flower." The four principal elements - oxygen, nitrogen, hydrogen, and carbon - say, "It is not in us, because we are from all eternity, and life is not; we form only its physical basis." Warmth and moisture say, "It is not in us; we are only its faithful nurses and handmaidens." The sun says: "It is not in me; I shine on dead worlds as well. I but quicken life after it is planted." The stars say, "It is not in us; we have seen life come and go among myriads of worlds for untold ages." No questioning of the heavens above nor of the earth below can reveal to us the secret we are in quest of.

I can fancy brute matter saying to life: "You tarry with me at your peril. You will always be on the firing-line of my blind, contending forces; they will respect you not; you must take your chances amid my flying missiles. My forces go their eternal round without variableness or shadow of turning, and woe to you if you cross their courses. You may bring all your gods with you - gods of love, mercy, gentleness, altruism; but I know them not. Your prayers will fall upon ears of stone, your appealing gesture upon eyes of stone, your cries for mercy upon hearts of stone. I shall be neither your enemy nor your friend. I shall be utterly indifferent to you. My floods will drown you, my winds wreck you, my fires burn you, my quicksands suck you down, and not know what they are doing. My earth is a theatre of storms and cyclones, of avalanches and earthquakes, of lightnings and cloudbursts; wrecks and ruins strew my course. All my elements and forces are at your service; all my fluids and gases and solids; my stars in their courses will fight on your side, if you put and keep yourself in right relations to them. My atoms and electrons will build your houses, my lightning do your errands, my winds sail your ships, on the same terms. You cannot live without my air and my water and my warmth; but each of them is a source of power that will crush or engulf or devour you before it will turn one hair's-breadth from its course. Your trees will be uprooted by my tornadoes, your fair fields will be laid waste by floods or fires; my mountains will fall on your delicate forms and utterly crush and bury them; my glaciers will overspread vast areas and banish or destroy whole tribes and races of your handiwork; the shrinking and wrinkling crust of my earth will fold in its insensate bosom vast forests of your tropical growths, and convert them into black rock, and I will make rock of the myriad forms of minute life with which you plant the seas; through immense geologic ages my relentless, unseeing, unfeeling forces will drive on like the ploughshare that buries every flower and grass-blade and tiny creature in its path. My winds are life-giving breezes to-day, and the besom of destruction to-morrow; my rains will moisten and nourish you one day, and wash you into the gulf the next; my earthquakes will bury your cities as if they were ant-hills. So you must take your chances, but the chances are on your side. I am not all tempest, or flood, or fire, or earthquake. Your career will be a warfare, but you will win more battles than you will lose. But remember, you are nothing to me, while I am everything to you. I have nothing to lose or gain, while you have everything to gain. Without my soils and moisture and warmth, without my carbon and oxygen and nitrogen and hydrogen, you can do or be nothing; without my sunshine you perish; but you have these things on condition of effort and struggle. You have evolution on condition of pain and failure and the hazard of the warring geologic ages. Fate and necessity rule in my realm. When you fail, or are crushed or swallowed by my remorseless forces, do not blame my gods, or your own; there is no blame, there is only the price to be paid: the hazards of invading the closed circle of my unseeing forces."

In California I saw an epitome of the merciless way inorganic Nature deals with life. An old, dried, and hardened asphalt lake near Los Angeles tells a horrible tale of animal suffering and failure. It had been a pit of horrors for long ages; it was Nature concentrated - her wild welter of struggling and devouring forms through the geologic ages made visible and tangible in a small patch of mingled pitch and animal bones. There was nearly as much bone as pitch. The fate of the unlucky flies that alight upon tangle-foot fly-paper in our houses had been the fate of the victims that had perished here. How many wild creatures had turned appealing eyes to the great unheeding void as they felt themselves helpless and sinking in this all-engulfing pitch! In like manner how many human beings in storms and disasters at sea and in flood and fire upon land have turned the same appealing look to the unpitying heavens! There is no power in the world of physical forces, or apart from our own kind, that heeds us or turns aside for us, or bestows one pitying glance upon us. Life has run, and still runs, the gantlet of a long line of hostile forces, and escapes by dint of fleetness of foot, or agility in dodging, or else by toughness of fibre.

Yet here we are; here is love and charity and mercy and intelligence; the fair face of childhood, the beautiful face of youth, the clear, strong face of manhood and womanhood, and the calm, benign face of old age, seen, it is true, as against a background of their opposites, but seeming to indicate something above chance and change at the heart of Nature. Here is life in the midst of death; but death forever playing into the hands of life; here is the organic in the midst of the inorganic, at strife with it, hourly crushed by it, yet sustained and kept going by its aid.

III

Vitality is only a word, but it marks a class of phenomena in nature that stands apart from all merely mechanical manifestations in the universe. The cosmos is a vast machine, but in this machine - this tremendous complex of physical forces - there appears, at least on this earth, in the course of its evolution, this something, or this peculiar manifestation of energy, that we call vital. Apparently it is a transient phase of activity in matter, which, unlike other chemical and physical activities, has its beginning and its ending, and out of which have arisen all the myriad forms of terrestrial life. The merely material forces, blind and haphazard from the first, did not arise in matter; they are inseparable from it; they are as eternal as matter itself; but the activities called vital arose in time and place, and must eventually disappear as they arose, while the career of the inorganic elements goes on as if life had never visited the sphere. Was it, or is it, a visitation - something *ab extra* that implies super-mundane, or supernatural, powers?

Added to this wonder is the fact that the vital order has gone on unfolding through the geologic ages, mounting from form to form, or from order to order, becoming more and more complex, passing from the emphasis of size of body, to the emphasis of size of brain, and finally from instinct and reflex activities to free volition, and the reason and consciousness of man; while the purely physical and chemical forces remain where they began. There has been endless change among them, endless shifting of the balance of power, but always the tendency to a dead equilibrium, while the genius of the organic forces has been in the power to disturb the equilibrium and to ride into port on the crest of the wave it has created, or to hang forever between the stable and the unstable.

So there we are, confronted by two apparently contrary truths. It is to me unthinkable that the vital order is not as truly rooted in the constitution of things as are the mechanical and chemical orders; and yet, here we are face to face with its limited, fugitive, or transitional character. It comes and goes like the dews of the morning; it has all the features of an exceptional, unexpected, extraordinary occurrence - of miracle, if you will; but if the light which physical science turns on the universe is not a delusion, if the habit of mind which it begets is not a false one, then life belongs to the same category of things as do day and night, rain and sun, rest and motion. Who shall reconcile these contradictions?

Huxley spoke for physical science when he said that he did not know what it was that constituted life - what it was that made the "wonderful difference between the dead particles and the living particles of matter appearing in other respects identical." He thought there might be some bond between physico-chemical phenomena, on the one hand, and vital phenomena, on the other, which philosophers will some day find out. Living matter is characterized by "spontaneity of action," which is entirely absent from inert matter. Huxley cannot or does not think of a vital force distinct from all other forces, as the cause of life phenomena, as so many philosophers have done, from Aristotle down to our day. He finds protoplasm to be the physical basis of life; it is one in both the vegetable and animal worlds; the animal takes it from the vegetable, and the vegetable, by the aid of sunlight, takes or manufactures it from the inorganic elements. But protoplasm is living matter. Before there was any protoplasm, what brought about the stupendous change of the dead into the living? Protoplasm makes more protoplasm, as fire makes more fire, but what kindled the first spark of this living flame? Here we corner the mystery, but it is still a mystery that defies us. Cause and effect meet and are lost in each other. Science cannot admit a miracle, or a break in the continuity of life, yet here it reaches a point where no step can be taken. Huxley's illustrations do not help his argument. "Protoplasm," he says, "is the clay of the potter; which, bake it and paint it as he will, remains clay, separated by artifice, and not by nature, from the commonest brick or sun-dried clod." Clay is certainly the physical basis of the potter's art, but would there be any pottery in the world if it contained only clay? Do we not have to think of the potter? In the same way, do we not have to think of something that fashions these myriad forms of life out of protoplasm? - and back of that, of something that begat protoplasm out of non-protoplasmic matter, and started the flame of life going? Life accounts for protoplasm, but what accounts for life? We have to think of the living clay as separated by Nature from the inert "sun-dried clod." There is something in the one that is not in the other. There is really no authentic analogy between the potter's art and Nature's art of life.

The force of the analogy, if it has any, drives us to the conclusion that life is an entity, or an agent, working upon matter and independent of it.

There is more wit than science in Huxley's question, "What better philosophical status has vitality than aquosity?" There is at least this difference: When vitality is gone, you cannot recall it, or reproduce it by your chemistry; but you can recombine the two gases in which you have decomposed water, any number of times, and get your aquosity back again; it never fails; it is a power of chemistry. But vitality will not come at your beck; it is not a chemical product, at least in the same sense that water is; it is not in the same category as the wetness or liquidity of water. It is a name for a phenomenon - the most remarkable phenomenon in nature. It is one that the art of man is powerless to reproduce, while water may be made to go through its cycle of change - solid, fluid, vapor, gas - and always come back to water. Well does the late Professor Brooks, of Johns Hopkins, say that "living things do, in some way and in some degree, control or condition inorganic nature; that they hold their own by setting the mechanical properties of matter in opposition to each other, and that this is their most notable and distinctive characteristic." Does not Ray Lankester, the irate champion of the mechanistic view of life, say essentially the same thing when he calls man the great Insurgent in Nature's camp - "crossing her courses, reversing her processes, and defeating her ends?"

Life appears like the introduction of a new element or force or tendency into the cosmos. Henceforth the elements go new ways, form new compounds, build up new forms, and change the face of nature. Rivers flow where they never would have flowed without it, mountains fall in a space of time during which they never would have fallen; barriers arise, rough ways are made smooth, a new world appears - the world of man's physical and mental activities.

If the gods of the inorganic elements are neither for nor against us, but utterly indifferent to us, how came we here? Nature's method is always from the inside, while ours is from the outside; hers is circular while ours is direct. We think, as Bergson says, of things created, and of a thing that creates, but things in nature are not created, they are evolved; they grow, and the thing that grows is not separable from the force that causes it to grow. The water turns the wheel, and can be shut off or let on. This is the way of the mechanical world. But the wheels in organic nature go around from something inside them, a kind of perpetual motion, or self-supplying power. They are not turned, they turn; they are not repaired, they repair. The nature of living things cannot be interpreted by the laws of mechanical and chemical things, though mechanics and chemistry play the visible, tangible part in them. If we must discard the notion of a vital force, we may, as Professor Hartog suggests, make use of the term "vital behavior."

Of course man tries everything by himself and his own standards. He knows no intelligence but his own, no prudence, no love, no mercy, no justice, no economy, but his own, no god but such a one as fits his conception.

In view of all these things, how man got here is a problem. Why the slender thread of his line of descent was not broken in the warrings and upheavals of the terrible geologic ages, what power or agent took a hand in furthering his development, is beyond the reach of our biologic science.

Man's is the only intelligence, as we understand the word, in the universe, and his intelligence demands something akin to intelligence in the nature from which he sprang.

VII

LIFE AND MIND

I

There are three kinds of change in the world in which we live - physical and mechanical change which goes on in time and place among the tangible bodies about us, chemical change which goes on in the world of hidden molecules and atoms of which bodies are composed, and vital change which involves the two former, but which also involves the mysterious principle or activity which we call life. Life comes and goes, but the physical and chemical orders remain. The vegetable and animal kingdoms wax and wane, or disappear entirely, but the physico-chemical forces are as indestructible as matter itself. This fugitive and evanescent character of life, the way it uses and triumphs over the material forces, setting up new chemical activities in matter, sweeping over the land-areas of the earth like a conflagration, lifting the inorganic elements up into myriads of changing and beautiful forms, instituting a vast number of new chemical processes and compounds, defying the laboratory to reproduce it or kindle its least spark - a flame that cannot exist without carbon and oxygen, but of which carbon and oxygen do not hold the secret, a fire reversed, building up instead of pulling down, in the vegetable with power to absorb and transmute the inorganic elements into leaves and fruit and tissue; in the animal with power to change the vegetable products into bone and muscle and nerve and brain, and finally into thought and consciousness; run by the solar energy and dependent upon it, yet involving something which the sunlight cannot give us; in short, an activity in matter, or in a limited part of matter, as real as the physico-chemical activity, but, unlike it, defying all analysis and explanation and all our attempts at synthesis. It is this character of life, I say, that so easily leads us to look upon it as something *ab extra*, or super-added to matter, and not an evolution from it. It has led Sir Oliver Lodge to conceive of life as a distinct entity, existing independent of matter, and it is this conception that gives the key to Henri Bergson's wonderful book, "Creative Evolution."

There is possibly or probably a fourth change in matter, physical in its nature, but much more subtle and mysterious than any of the physical changes which our senses reveal to us. I refer to radioactive change, or to the atomic transformation of one element into another, such as the change of radium into helium, and the change of helium into lead - a subject that takes us to the borderland between physics and chemistry where is still debatable ground.

I began by saying that there were three kinds of changes in matter - the physical, the chemical, and the vital. But if we follow up this idea and declare that there are three kinds of force also, claiming this distinction for the third term of our proposition, we shall be running counter to the main current of recent biological science. "The idea that a peculiar 'vital force' acts in the chemistry of life," says Professor Soddy, "is extinct."

"Only chemical and physical agents influence the vital processes," says Professor Czapek, of the University of Prague, "and we need no longer take refuge in mysterious 'vital forces' when we want to explain these."

Tyndall was obliged to think of a force that guided the molecules of matter into the special forms of a tree. This force was in the ultimate particles of matter. But when he came to

John Burroughs

the brain and to consciousness, he said a new product appeared that defies mechanical treatment.

The attempt of the biological science of our time to wipe out all distinctions between the living and the non-living, solely because scientific analysis reveals no difference, is a curious and interesting phenomenon.

Professor Schaefer, in his presidential address before the British Association in 1912, argued that all the main characteristics of living matter, such as assimilation and disassimilation, growth and reproduction, spontaneous and amoeboid movement, osmotic pressure, karyokinesis, etc., were equally apparent in the non-living; therefore he concluded that life is only one of the many chemical reactions, and that it is not improbable that it will yet be produced by chemical synthesis in the laboratory. The logic of the position taken by Professor Schaefer and of the school to which he belongs, demands this artificial production of life - an achievement that seems no nearer than it did a half-century ago. When it has been attained, the problem will be simplified, but the mystery of life will by no means have been cleared up. One follows these later biochemists in working out their problem of the genesis of life with keen interest, but always with a feeling that there is more in their conclusions than is justified by their premises. For my own part, I am convinced that whatever is, is natural, but to obtain life I feel the need of something of a different order from the force that evokes the spark from the flint and the steel, or brings about the reaction of chemical compounds. If asked to explain what this something is that is characteristic of living matter, I should say intelligence.

The new school of biologists start with matter that possesses extraordinary properties - with matter that seems inspired with the desire for life, and behaving in a way that it never will behave in the laboratory. They begin with the earth's surface warm and moist, the atmosphere saturated with watery vapor and carbon dioxide and many other complex unstable compounds; then they summon all the material elements of life - carbon, oxygen, hydrogen, and nitrogen, with a little sodium, chlorine, iron, sulphur, phosphorus, and others - and make these run together to form a jelly-like body called a colloid; then they endow this jelly mass with the power of growth, and of subdivision when it gets too large; they make it able to absorb various unstable compounds from the air, giving it internal stores of energy, "the setting free of which would cause automatic movements in the lump of jelly." Thus they lay the foundations of life. This carbonaceous material with properties of movement and subdivision due to mechanical and physical forces is the immediate ancestor of the first imaginary living being, the *protobion*. To get this *protobion* the chemists summon a reagent known as a catalyser. The catalyser works its magic on the jelly mass. It sets up a wonderful reaction by its mere presence, without parting with any of its substance. Thus, if a bit of platinum which has this catalytic power is dropped into a vessel containing a mixture of oxygen and hydrogen, the two gases instantly unite and form water. A catalyser introduced in the primordial jelly liberates energy and gives the substance power to break up the various complex unstable compounds into food, and promote growth and subdivision. In fact, it awakens or imparts a vital force and leads to "indefinite increase, subdivision, and movement."

With Professor Schaefer there is first "the fortuitous production of life upon this globe" - the chance meeting or jostling of the elements that resulted in a bit of living protoplasm, "or a mass of colloid slime" in the old seas, or on their shores, "possessing the property of assimilation and therefore of growth." Here the whole mystery is swallowed at one gulp. "Reproduction would follow as a matter of course," because all material of this physical nature - fluid or semi-fluid in character - "has a tendency to undergo subdivision when its bulk exceeds a certain size."

"A mass of colloidal slime" that has the power of assimilation and of growth and reproduction, is certainly a new thing in the world, and no chemical analysis of it can clear up the mystery. It is easy enough to produce colloidal slime, but to endow it with these wonderful powers so that "the promise and the potency of all terrestrial life" slumbers in it is a staggering proposition.

Whatever the character of this subdivision, whether into equal parts or in the form of buds, "every separate part would resemble the parent in chemical and physical properties, and would equally possess the property of taking in and assimilating suitable material from its liquid environment, growing in bulk and reproducing its like by subdivision. In this way from any beginning of living material a primitive form of life would spread and would gradually people the globe. The establishment of life being once effected, all forms of organization follow under the inevitable laws of evolution." Why all forms of organization - why the body and brain of man - must inevitably follow from the primitive bit of living matter, is just the question upon which we want light. The proposition begs the question. Certainly when you have got the evolutionary process once started in matter which has these wonderful powers, all is easy. The professor simply describes what has taken place and seems to think that the mystery is thereby cleared up, as if by naming all the parts of a machine and their relation to one another, the machine is accounted for. What caused the iron and steel and wood of the machine to take this special form, while in other cases the iron and steel and wood took other radically different forms, and vast quantities of these substances took no form at all?

In working out the evolution of living forms by the aid of the blind physical and chemical agents alone, Professor Schaefer unconsciously ascribes the power of choice and purpose to the individual cells, as when he says that the cells of the external layer sink below the surface for better protection and better nutrition. It seems to have been a matter of choice or will that the cells developed a nervous system in the animal and not in the vegetable. Man came because a few cells in some early form of life acquired a slightly greater tendency to react to an external stimulus. In this way they were brought into closer touch with the outer world and thereby gained the lead of their duller neighbor cells, and became the real rulers of the body, and developed the mind.

It is bewildering to be told by so competent a person as Professor Schaefer that at bottom there is no fundamental difference between the living and non-living. We need not urge the existence of a peculiar vital force, as distinct from all other forces, but all distinctions between things are useless if we cannot say that a new behavior is set up in matter which we describe by the word "vital," and that a new principle is operative in organized matter which we must call "intelligence." Of course all movements and processes of living beings are in conformity with the general laws of matter, but does such a statement necessarily rule out all idea of the operation of an organizing and directing principle that is not operative in the world of inanimate things?

In Schaefer's philosophy evolution is purely a mechanical process - there is no inborn tendency, no inherent push, no organizing effort, but all results from the blind groping and chance jostling of the inorganic elements; from the molecules of undifferentiated protoplasm to the brain of a Christ or a Plato, is just one series of unintelligent physical and chemical activities in matter.

May we not say that all the marks or characteristics of a living body which distinguish it in our experience from an inanimate body, are of a non-scientific character, or outside the sphere of experimental science? We recognize them as readily as we distinguish day from night, but we cannot describe them in the fixed terms of science. When we say growth, metabolism, osmosis, the colloidal state, science points out that all this may be affirmed of inorganic bodies. When we say a life principle, a vital force or soul or spirit or intelligence, science turns a deaf ear.

The difference between the living and the non-living is not so much a physical difference as a metaphysical difference. Living matter is actuated by intelligence. Its activities are spontaneous and self-directing. The rock, and the tree that grows beside it, and the insects and rodents that burrow under it, may all be made of one stuff, but their difference to the beholder is fundamental; there is an intelligent activity in the one that is not in the other. Now no scientific analysis of a body will reveal the secret of this activity. As well might your analysis of a phonographic record hope to disclose a sonata of Beethoven latent in the waving lines. No power of chemistry could reveal any difference between the gray matter of Plato's brain and that of the humblest citizen of Athens. All the difference between man, all that makes a man a man, and an ox an ox, is beyond the reach of any of your physico-chemical tests. By the same token the gulf that separates the organic from the inorganic is not within the power of science to disclose. The biochemist is bound to put life in the category of the material forces because his science can deal with no other. To him the word "vital" is a word merely, it stands for no reality, and the secret of life is merely a chemical reaction. A living body awakens a train of ideas in our minds that a non-living fails to awaken - a train of ideas that belong to another order from that awakened by scientific demonstration. We cannot blame science for ruling out that which it cannot touch with its analysis, or repeat with its synthesis. The phenomena of life are as obvious to us as anything in the world; we know their signs and ways, and witness their power, yet in the alembic of our science they turn out to be only physico-chemical processes; hence that is all there is of them. Vitality, says Huxley, has no more reality than the horology of a clock. Yet Huxley sees three equal realities in the universe - matter, energy, and consciousness. But consciousness is the crown of a vital process. Hence it would seem as if there must be something more real in vitality than Huxley is willing to admit.

II

Nearly all the later biologists or biological philosophers are as
shy of the term "vital force," and even of the word "vitality," as
they are of the words "soul," "spirit," "intelligence," when
discussing natural phenomena. To experimental science such
words have no meaning because the supposed realities for
which they stand are quite beyond the reach of scientific
analysis. Ray Lankester, in his "Science from an Easy Chair,"
following Huxley, compares vitality with aquosity, and says
that to have recourse to a vital principle or force to explain a
living body is no better philosophy than to appeal to a
principle of aquosity to explain water. Of course words are
words, and they have such weight with us that when we have
got a name for a thing it is very easy to persuade ourselves that
the thing exists. The terms "vitality," "vital force," have long
been in use, and it is not easy to convince one's self that they
stand for no reality. Certain it is that living and non-living
matter are sharply separated, though when reduced to their
chemical constituents in the laboratory they are found to be
identical. The carbon, the hydrogen, the nitrogen, the oxygen,
and the lime, sulphur, iron, etc., in a living body are in no way
peculiar, but are the same as these elements in the rocks and
the soil. We are all made of one stuff; a man and his dog are
made of one stuff; an oak and a pine are made of one stuff; Jew
and Gentile are made of one stuff. Should we be justified,
then, in saying that there is no difference between them? There
is certainly a moral and an intellectual difference between a
man and his dog, if there is no chemical and mechanical
difference. And there is as certainly as wide or a wider
difference between living and non-living matter, though it be
beyond the reach of science to detect. For this difference we
have to have a name, and we use the words "vital," "vitality,"
which seem to me to stand for as undeniable realities as the
words heat, light, chemical affinity, gravitation. There is not a
principle of roundness, though "nature centres into balls," nor
of squareness, though crystallization is in right lines, nor of
aquosity, though two thirds of the surface of the earth is

covered with water. Can we on any better philosophical grounds say that there is a principle of vitality, though the earth swarms with living beings? Yet the word vitality stands for a reality, it stands for a peculiar activity in matter - for certain movements and characteristics for which we have no other term. I fail to see any analogy between aquosity and that condition of matter we call vital or living. Aquosity is not an activity, it is a property, the property of wetness; viscosity is a term to describe other conditions of matter; solidity, to describe still another condition; and opacity and transparency, to describe still others - as they affect another of our senses. But the vital activity in matter is a concrete reality. With it there goes the organizing tendency or impulse, and upon it hinges the whole evolutionary movement of the biological history of the globe. We can do all sorts of things with water and still keep its aquosity. If we resolve it into its constituent gases we destroy its aquosity, but by uniting these gases chemically we have the wetness back again. But if a body loses its vitality, its life, can we by the power of chemistry, or any other power within our reach, bring the vitality back to it? Can we make the dead live? You may bray your living body in a mortar, destroy every one of its myriad cells, and yet you may not extinguish the last spark of life; the protoplasm is still living. But boil it or bake it and the vitality is gone, and all the art and science of mankind cannot bring it back again. The physical and chemical activities remain after the vital activities have ceased. Do we not then have to supply a non-chemical, a non-physical force or factor to account for the living body? Is there no difference between the growth of a plant or an animal, and the increase in size of a sand-bank or a snow-bank, or a river delta? or between the wear and repair of a working-man's body and the wear and repair of the machine he drives? Excretion and secretion are not in the same categories. The living and the non-living mark off the two grand divisions of matter in the world in which we live, as no two terms merely descriptive of chemical and physical phenomena ever can. Life is a motion in matter, but of another order from that of the physico-chemical, though inseparable from it. We may forego the convenient term "vital force." Modern science shies at the term "force." We must have force or energy or pressure of some kind to lift dead matter up into the myriad forms of life, though in the last analysis of it it may all date from the sun. When it builds a living body, we call it a vital force; when it builds a gravel-bank, or moves a glacier, we call it a mechanical force; when it writes a poem or composes a symphony, we call it a psychic force - all distinctions which we cannot well dispense with, though of the ultimate reality for which these terms stand we can know little. In the latest science heat and light are not substances, though electricity is. They are peculiar motions in matter which give rise to sensations in certain living bodies that we name light and heat, as another peculiar motion in matter gives rise to a sensation we call sound. Life is another kind of motion in certain aggregates of matter - more mysterious or inexplicable than all others because it cannot be described in terms of the others, and because it defies the art and science of man to reproduce.

Though the concepts "vital force" and "life principle" have no standing in the court of modern biological science, it is interesting to observe how often recourse is had by biological writers to terms that embody the same idea. Thus the German physiologist Verworn, the determined enemy of the old conception of life, in his great work on "Irritability," has recourse to "the specific energy of living substances." One is forced to believe that without this "specific energy" his "living substances" would never have arisen out of the non-living.

Professor Moore, of Liverpool University, as I have already pointed out while discussing the term "vital force," invents a new phrase, "biotic energy," to explain the same phenomena. Surely a force by any other name is no more and no less potent. Both Verworn and Moore feel the need, as we all do, of some term, or terms, by which to explain that activity in matter which we call vital. Other writers have referred to "a peculiar power of synthesis" in plants and animals, which the inanimate forms do not possess.

Ray Lankester, to whom I have already referred in discussing this subject, helps himself out by inventing, not a new force, but a new substance in which he fancies "resides the peculiar property of living matter." He calls this hypothetical substance "plasmogen," and thinks of it as an ultimate chemical compound hidden in protoplasm. Has this "ultimate molecule of life" any more scientific or philosophical validity than the old conception of a vital force? It looks very much like another name for the same thing - an attempt to give the mind something to take hold of in dealing with the mystery of living things. This imaginary "life-stuff" of the British scientist is entirely beyond the reach of chemical analysis; no man has ever seen it or proved its existence. In fact it is simply an invention of Ray Lankester to fill a break in the sequence of observed phenomena. Something seems to possess the power of starting or kindling that organizing activity in a living body, and it seems to me it matters little whether we call it "plasmogen," or a "life principle," or "biotic energy," or what not; it surely leavens the loaf. Matter takes on new activities under its influence. Ray Lankester thinks that plasmogen came into being in early geologic ages, and that the conditions which led to its formation have probably never recurred. Whether he thinks its formation was merely a chance hit or not, he does not say.

We see matter all about us, acted upon by the mechanico-chemical forces, that never takes on any of the distinctive phenomena of living bodies. Yet Verworn is convinced that if we could bring the elements of a living body together as Nature does, in the same order and proportion, and combine them in the selfsame way, or bring about the vital conditions, a living being would result. Undoubtedly. It amounts to saying that if we had Nature's power we could do what she does. *If* we could marry the elements as she does, and bless the banns as she seems to, we could build a man out of a clay-bank. But clearly physics and chemistry alone, as we know and practice them, are not equal to the task.

III

One of the fundamental characteristics of life is power of adaptation; it will adapt itself to almost any condition; it is willing and accommodating. It is like a stream that can be turned into various channels; the gall insects turn it into channels to suit their ends when they sting the leaf of a tree or the stalk of a plant, and deposit an egg in the wound. "Build me a home and a nursery for my young," says the insect. "With all my heart," says the leaf, and forthwith forgets its function as a leaf, and proceeds to build up a structure, often of great delicacy and complexity, to house and cradle its enemy. The current of life flows on blindly and takes any form imposed upon it. But in the case of the vegetable galls it takes life to control life. Man cannot produce these galls by artificial means. But we can take various mechanical and chemical liberties with embryonic animal life in its lower sea-forms. Professor Loeb has fertilized the eggs of sea-urchins by artificial means. The eggs of certain forms may be made to produce twins by altering the constitution of the sea-water, and the twins can be made to grow together so as to produce monstrosities by another chemical change in the sea-water. The eyes of certain fish embryos may be fused into a single cyclopean eye by adding magnesium chloride to the water in which they live. Loeb says, "It is *a priori* obvious that an unlimited number of pathological variations might be produced by a variation in the concentration and constitution of the sea water, and experience confirms this statement." It has been found that when frog's eggs are turned upside down and compressed between two glass plates for a number of hours, some of the eggs give rise to twins. Professor Morgan found that if he destroyed half of a frog's egg after the first segmentation, the remaining half gave rise to half an embryo, but that if he put the half-egg upside down, and compressed it between two glass plates, he got a perfect embryo frog of half the normal size. Such things show how plastic and adaptive life is. Dr. Carrel's experiments with living animal tissue immersed in a proper mother-liquid illustrate how the vital process -

cell-multiplication - may be induced to go on and on, blindly, aimlessly, for an almost indefinite time. The cells multiply, but they do not organize themselves into a constructive community and build an organ or any purposeful part. They may be likened to a lot of blind masons piling up brick and mortar without any architect to direct their work or furnish them a plan. A living body of the higher type is not merely an association of cells; it is an association and cooeperation of communities of cells, each community working to a definite end and building an harmonious whole. The biochemist who would produce life in the laboratory has before him the problem of compounding matter charged with this organizing tendency or power, and doubtless if he ever should evoke this mysterious process through his chemical reactions, it would possess this power, as this is what distinguishes the organic from the inorganic.

I do not see mind or intelligence in the inorganic world in the sense in which I see it in the organic. In the heavens one sees power, vastness, sublimity, unspeakable, but one sees only the physical laws working on a grander scale than on the earth. Celestial mechanics do not differ from terrestrial mechanics, however tremendous and imposing the result of their activities. But in the humblest living thing - in a spear of grass by the roadside, in a gnat, in a flea - there lurks a greater mystery. In an animate body, however small, there abides something of which we get no trace in the vast reaches of astronomy, a kind of activity that is incalculable, indeterminate, and super-mechanical, not lawless, but making its own laws, and escaping from the iron necessity that rules in the inorganic world.

Our mathematics and our science can break into the circle of the celestial and the terrestrial forces, and weigh and measure and separate them, and in a degree understand them; but the forces of life defy our analysis as well as our synthesis.

Knowing as we do all the elements that make up the body and brain of a man, all the physiological processes, and all the relations and interdependence of his various organs, if, in addition, we knew all his inheritances, his whole ancestry back to the primordial cells from which he sprang, and if we also knew that of every person with whom he comes in contact and who influences his life, could we forecast his future, predict the orbit in which his life would revolve, indicate its eclipses, its perturbations, and the like, as we do that of an astronomic body? or could we foresee his affinities and combinations as we do that of a chemical body? Had we known any of the animal forms in his line of ascent, could we have foretold man as we know him to-day? Could we have foretold the future of any form of life from its remote beginnings? Would our mathematics and our chemistry have been of any avail in our dealing with such a problem? Biology is not in the same category with geology and astronomy. In the inorganic world, chemical affinity builds up and pulls down. It integrates the rocks and, under changed conditions, it disintegrates them. In the organic world chemical affinity is equally active, but it plays a subordinate part. It neither builds up nor pulls down. Vital activities, if we must shun the term "vital force," do both. Barring accidents, the life of all organisms is terminated by other organisms. In the order of nature, life destroys life, and compounds destroy compounds. When the air and soil and water hold no invisible living germs, organic bodies never decay. It is not the heat that begets putrefaction, but germs in the air. Sufficient heat kills the germs, but what disintegrates the germs and reduces them to dust? Other still smaller organisms? and so on *ad infinitum*? Does the sequence of life have no end? The destruction of one chemical compound means the formation of other chemical compounds; chemical affinity cannot be annulled, but the activity we call vital is easily arrested. A living body can be killed, but a chemical body can only be changed into another chemical body.

The least of living things, I repeat, holds a more profound mystery than all our astronomy and our geology hold. It introduces us to activities which our mathematics do not help us to deal with. Our science can describe the processes of a living body, and name all the material elements that enter into it, but it cannot tell us in what the peculiar activity consists, or just what it is that differentiates living matter from non-living. Its analysis reveals no difference. But this difference consists in something beyond the reach of chemistry and of physics; it is active intelligence, the power of self-direction, of self-adjustment, of self-maintenance, of adapting means to an end. It is notorious that the hand cannot always cover the flea; this atom has will, and knows the road to safety. Behold what our bodies know over and above what we know! Professor Czapek reveals to us a chemist at work in the body who proceeds precisely like the chemist in his laboratory; they might both have graduated at the same school. Thus the chemist in the laboratory is accustomed to dissolve the substance which is to be used in an experiment to react on other substances. The chemical course in living cells is the same. All substances destined for reactions are first dissolved. No compound is taken up in living cells before it is dissolved. Digestion is essentially identical with dissolving or bringing into a liquid state. On the other hand, when the chemist wishes to preserve a living substance from chemical change, he transfers it from a state of solution into a solid state. The chemist in the living body does the same thing. Substances which are to be stored up, such as starch, fat, or protein bodies, are deposited in insoluble form, ready to be dissolved and used whenever wanted for the life processes. Poisonous substances are eliminated from living bodies by the same process of precipitation. Oxalic acid is a product of oxidation in living cells, and has strong poisonous properties. To get rid of it, the chemist inside the body, by the aid of calcium salts, forms insoluble compounds of it, and thus casts it out. To separate substances from each other by filtration, or by shaking with suitable liquids, is one of the daily tasks of the chemist. Analogous processes occur regularly in living cells. Again, when the chemist wishes to finish his filtration quickly, he uses filters which have a large surface. "In living protoplasms, this condition is very well fulfilled by the foam-like structure which affords an immense surface in a very small space." In the laboratory the chemist mixes his substances by stirring. The body chemist achieves the same result by the streaming of protoplasm. The cells know what they want, and how to attain it, as clearly as the chemist does. The intelligence of the living body, or what we must call such for want of a better term, is shown in scores of ways - by the means it takes to protect itself against microbes, by the antitoxins that it forms. Indeed, if we knew all that our bodies know, what mysteries would be revealed to us!

John Burroughs

IV

Life goes up-stream - goes against the tendency to a static equilibrium in matter; decay and death go down. What is it in the body that struggles against poisons and seeks to neutralize their effects? What is it that protects the body against a second attack of certain diseases, making it immune? Chemical changes, undoubtedly, but what brings about the chemical changes? The body is a *colony* of living units called cells, that behaves much like a colony of insects when it takes measures to protect itself against its enemies. The body forms anti-toxins when it has to. It knows how to do it as well as bees know how to ventilate the hive, or how to seal up or entomb the grub of an invading moth. Indeed, how much the act of the body, in encysting a bullet in its tissues, is like the act of the bees in encasing with wax a worm in the combs!

What is that in the body which at great altitudes increases the number of red corpuscles in the blood, those oxygen-bearers, so as to make up for the lessened amount of oxygen breathed by reason of the rarity of the air? Under such conditions, the amount of haemoglobin is almost doubled. I do not call this thing a force; I call it an intelligence - the intelligence that pervades the body and all animate nature, and does the right thing at the right time. We, no doubt, speak too loosely of it when we say that it prompts or causes the body to do this, or to do that; it *is* the body; the relation of the two has no human analogy; the two are one.

Man breaks into the circuit of the natural inorganic forces and arrests them and controls them, and makes them do his work - turn his wheels, drive his engines, run his errands, etc.; but he cannot do this in the same sense with the organic forces; he cannot put a spell upon the pine tree and cause it to build him a house or a nursery. Only the insects can do a thing like that; only certain insects can break into the circuit of vegetable life and divert its forces to serve their special ends. One kind of an insect stings a bud or a leaf of the oak, and the tree forthwith grows a solid nutlike protuberance the size of a chestnut, in which the larvae of the insect live and feed and mature. Another insect stings the same leaf and produces the common oak-apple - a smooth, round, green, shell-like body filled with a network of radiating filaments, with the egg and then the grub of the insect at the centre. Still another kind of insect stings the oak bud and deposits its eggs there, and the oak proceeds to grow a large white ball made up of a kind of succulent vegetable wool with red spots evenly distributed over its surface, as if it were some kind of spotted fruit or flower. In June, it is about the size of a small apple. Cut it in half and you find scores of small shell-like growths radiating from the bud-stem, like the seeds of the dandelion, each with a kind of vegetable pappus rising from it, and together making up the ball as the pappus of the dandelion seeds makes up the seed-globe of this plant. It is one of the most singular vegetable products, or vegetable perversions, that I know of. A sham fruit filled with sham seeds; each seed-like growth contains a grub, which later in the season pupates and eats its way out, a winged insect. How foreign to anything we know as mechanical or chemical it all is! - the surprising and incalculable tricks of life!

Another kind of insect stings the oak leaf and there develops a pale, smooth, solid, semi-transparent sphere, the size of a robin's egg, dense and succulent like the flesh of an apple, with the larvae of the insect subsisting in its interior. Each of these widely different forms is evoked from the oak leaf by the magic of an insect's ovipositor. Chemically, the constituents of all of them are undoubtedly the same.

It is one of the most curious and suggestive things in living nature. It shows how plastic and versatile life is, and how utterly unmechanical. Life plays so many and such various tunes upon the same instruments; or rather, the living organism is like many instruments in one; the tones of all instruments slumber in it to be awakened when the right performer appears. At least four different insects get four different tunes, so to speak, out of the oak leaf.

Certain insects avail themselves of the animal organism also and go through their cycle of development and metamorphosis within its tissues or organs in a similar manner.

V

On the threshold of the world of living organisms stands that wonderful minute body, the cell, the unit of life - a piece of self-regulating and self-renewing mechanism that holds the key to all the myriads of living forms that fill the world, from the amoeba up to man. For chemistry to produce the cell is apparently as impossible as for it to produce a bird's egg, or a living flower, or the heart and brain of man. The body is a communal state made up of myriads of cells that all work together to build up and keep going the human personality. There is the same cooeeperation and division of labor that takes place in the civic state, and in certain insect communities. As in the social and political organism, thousands of the citizen cells die every day and new cells of the same kind take their place. Or, it is like an army in battle being constantly recruited - as fast as a soldier falls another takes his place, till the whole army is changed, and yet remains the same. The waste is greatest at the surface of the body through the skin, and through the stomach and lungs. The worker cells, namely, the tissue cells, like the worker bees in the hive, pass away the most rapidly; then, according to Haeckel, there are certain constants, certain cells that remain throughout life. "There is always a solid groundwork of conservative cells, the descendants of which secure the further regeneration." The traditions of the state are kept up by the citizen-cells that remain, so that, though all is changed in time, the genius of the state remains; the individuality of the man is not lost. "The sense of personal identity is maintained across the flight of molecules," just as it is maintained in the state or nation, by the units that remain, and by the established order. There is an unwritten constitution, a spirit that governs, like Maeterlinck's "spirit of the hive." The traditions of the body are handed down from mother cell to daughter cell, though just what that means in terms of physiology or metabolism I do not know. But this we know - that you are you and I am I, and that human life and personality can never be fully explained or accounted for in terms of the material forces.

VIII

LIFE AND SCIENCE

I

The limited and peculiar activity which arises in matter and which we call vital; which comes and goes; which will not stay to be analyzed; which we in vain try to reproduce in our laboratories; which is inseparable from chemistry and physics, but which is not summed up by them; which seems to use them and direct them to new ends, - an entity which seems to have invaded the kingdom of inert matter at some definite time in the earth's history, and to have set up an insurgent movement there; cutting across the circuits of the mechanical and chemical forces; turning them about, pitting one against the other; availing itself of gravity, of chemical affinity, of fluids and gases, of osmosis and exosmosis, of colloids, of oxidation and hydration, and yet explicable by none of these things; clothing itself with garments of warmth and color and perfume woven from the cold, insensate elements; setting up new activities in matter; building up myriads of new unstable compounds; struggling against the tendency of the physical forces to a dead equilibrium; indeterminate, intermittent, fugitive; limited in time, limited in space; present in some worlds, absent from others; breaking up the old routine of the material forces, and instituting new currents, new tendencies; departing from the linear activities of the inorganic, and setting up the circular activities of living currents; replacing change by metamorphosis, revolution by evolution, accretion by secretion, crystallization by cell-formation, aggregation by growth; and, finally, introducing a new power into the world - the mind and soul of man - this wonderful, and apparently transcendental something which we call life - how baffling and yet how fascinating is the inquiry into its nature and origin! Are we to regard it as Tyndall did, and as others before and since his time did and do, as potential in the constitution of matter, and self-evolved, like the chemical compounds that are involved in its processes?

As mechanical energy is latent in coal, and in all combustible bodies, is vital energy latent in carbon, hydrogen, oxygen, and so forth, needing only the right conditions to bring it out? Mechanical energy is convertible into electrical energy, and *vice versa*. Indeed, the circle of the physical forces is easily traced, easily broken into, but when or how these forces merge into the vital and psychic forces, or support them, or become them - there is the puzzle. If we limit the natural to the inorganic order, then are living bodies supernatural? Super-mechanical and super-chemical certainly, and chemics and mechanics and electro-statics include all the material forces. Is life outside this circle? It is certain that this circle does not always include life, but can life exist outside this circle? When it appears it is always inside it.

Science can only deal with life as a physical phenomenon; as a psychic phenomenon it is beyond its scope, except so far as the psychic is manifested through the physical. Not till it has produced living matter from dead can it speak with authority upon the question of the origin of life. Its province is limited to the description and analysis of life processes, but when it essays to name what institutes the processes, or to disclose the secret of organization, it becomes philosophy or theology. When Haeckel says that life originated spontaneously, he does not speak with the authority of science, because he cannot prove his assertion; it is his opinion, and that is all. When Helmholtz says that life had no beginning, he is in the same case. When our later biophysicists say that life is of

John Burroughs

physico-chemical origin, they are in the same case; when Tyndall says that there is no energy in the universe but solar energy, he is in the same case; when Sir Oliver Lodge says that life is an entity outside of and independent of matter, he is in the same case. Philosophy and theology can take leaps in the dark, but science must have solid ground to go upon. When it speculates or theorizes, it must make its speculations good. Scientific prophecy is amenable to the same tests as other prophecy. In the absence of proof by experiment - scientific proof - to get the living out of the non-living we have either got to conceive of matter itself as fundamentally creative, as the new materialism assumes, or else we have got to have an external Creator, as the old theology assumes. And the difference is more apparent than real. Tyndall is "baffled and bewildered" by the fact that out of its molecular vibrations and activities "things so utterly incongruous with them as sensation, thought, and emotion can be derived." His science is baffled and bewildered because it cannot, bound as it is by the iron law of the conservation and correlation of energy, trace the connection between them. But his philosophy or his theology would experience little difficulty. Henri Bergson shows no hesitation in declaring that the fate of consciousness is not involved in the fate of the brain through which it is manifested, but it is his philosophy and not his science that inspires this faith. Tyndall deifies matter to get life out of it - makes the creative energy potential in it. Bergson deifies or spiritualizes life as a psychic, creative principle, and makes matter its instrument or vehicle.

Science is supreme in its own sphere, the sphere, or hemisphere, of the objective world, but it does not embrace the whole of human life, because human life is made up of two spheres, or hemispheres, one of which is the subjective world. There is a world within us also, the world of our memories, thoughts, emotions, aspirations, imaginings, which overarches the world of our practical lives and material experience, as the sky overarches the earth. It is in the spirit of science that we conquer and use the material world in which we live; it is in the spirit of art and literature, philosophy and religion, that we explore and draw upon the immaterial world of our own hearts and souls. Of course the man of science is also a philosopher - may I not even say he is also a prophet and poet? Not otherwise could he organize his scientific facts and see their due relations, see their drift and the sequence of forces that bind the universe into a whole. As a man of science he traces out the causes of the tides and the seasons, the nature and origin of disease, and a thousand and one other things; but only as a philosopher can he see the body as a whole and speculate about the mystery of its organization; only as a philosopher can he frame theories and compare values and interpret the phenomena he sees about him.

John Burroughs

II

We can only know, in the scientific sense, the physical and chemical phenomena of life; its essence, its origin, we can only know as philosophy and idealism know them. We have to turn philosophers when we ask any ultimate question. The feeling we have that the scientific conception of life is inadequate springs from the philosophical habit of mind. Yet this habit is quite as legitimate as the scientific habit, and is bound to supplement the latter all through life.

The great men of science, like Darwin and Huxley, are philosophers in their theories and conclusions, and men of science in their observations and experiments. The limitations of science in dealing with such a problem are seen in the fact that science can take no step till it has life to begin with. When it has got the living body, it can analyze its phenomena and reduce them to their chemical and physical equivalents, and thus persuade itself that the secret of life may yet be hit upon in the laboratory. Professor Czapek, of the University of Prague, in his work on "The Chemical Phenomena of Life" speaks for science when he says, "What we call life is nothing else but a complex of innumerable chemical reactions in the living substance which we call protoplasm." The "living substance" is assumed to begin with, and then we are told that the secret of its living lies in its chemical and physical processes. This is in one sense true. No doubt at all that if these processes were arrested, life would speedily end, but do they alone account for its origin? Is it not like accounting for a baby in terms of its breathing and eating? It was a baby before it did either, and it would seem as if life must in some way ante-date the physical and chemical processes that attend it, or at least be bound up in them in a way that no scientific analysis can reveal.

If life is merely a mode of motion in matter, it is fundamentally unlike any and all other modes of motion, because, while we can institute all the others at will, we are powerless to institute this. The mode of motion we call heat is going on in varying degrees of velocity all about us at all times and seasons, but the vital motion of matter is limited to a comparatively narrow circle. We can end it, but we cannot start it.

The rigidly scientific type of mind sees no greater mystery in the difference in contour of different animal bodies than a mere difference in the density of the germ cells: "one density results in a sequence of cell-densities to form a horse; another a dog; another a cat"; and avers that if we "repeat the same complex conditions, the same results are as inevitable as the sequences of forces that result in the formation of hydrogen monoxide from hydrogen and oxygen."

Different degrees of density may throw light on the different behavior of gases and fluids and solids, but can it throw any light on the question of why a horse is a horse, and a dog a dog? or why one is an herbivorous feeder, and the other a carnivorous?

The scientific explanation of life phenomena is analogous to reducing a living body to its ashes and pointing to them - the lime, the iron, the phosphorus, the hydrogen, the oxygen, the carbon, the nitrogen - as the whole secret.

Professor Czapek is not entirely consistent. He says that it is his conviction that there is something in physiology that transcends the chemistry and the physics of inorganic nature. At the same time he affirms, "It becomes more and more improbable that Life develops forces which are unknown in inanimate Nature." But psychic forces are a product of life, and they certainly are not found in inanimate nature. But without laying stress upon this fact, may we not say that if no new force is developed by, or is characteristic of, life, certainly new effects, new processes, new compounds of matter are produced by life? Matter undergoes some change that chemical analysis does not reveal. The mystery of isomeric substances appears, a vast number of new compounds of carbon appear, the face of the earth changes. The appearance of life in inert matter is a change analogous to the appearance of the mind of man in animate nature. The old elements and forces are turned to new and higher uses. Man does not add to the list of forces or elements in the earth, but he develops them, and turns them to new purposes; they now obey and serve him, just as the old chemistry and physics obey and serve life. Czapek tells us of the vast number of what are called enzymes, or ferments, that appear in living bodies - "never found in inorganic Nature and not to be gained by chemical synthesis." Orders and suborders of enzymes, they play a part in respiration, in digestion, in assimilation. Some act on the fats, some on the carbohydrates, some produce inversion, others dissolution and precipitation. These enzymes are at once the products and the agents of life. They must exert force, chemical force, or, shall we say, they transform chemical force into life force, or, to use Professor Moore's term, into "biotic energy"?

III

The inorganic seems dreaming of the organic. Behold its dreams in the fern and tree forms upon the window pane and upon the stone flagging of a winter morning! In the Brunonian movement of matter in solution, in crystallization, in chemical affinity, in polarity, in osmosis, in the growth of flint or chert nodules, in limestone formations - like seeking like - in these and in other activities, inert matter seems dreaming of life.

The chemists have played upon this tendency in the inorganic to parody or simulate some of the forms of living matter. A noted European chemist, Dr. Leduc, has produced what he calls "osmotic growths," from purely unorganized mineral matter - growths in form like seaweed and polyps and corals and trees. His seeds are fragments of calcium chloride, and his soil is a solution of the alkaline carbonates, phosphates, or silicates. When his seeds are sown in these solutions, we see inert matter germinating, "putting forth bud and stem and root and branch and leaf and fruit," precisely as in the living vegetable kingdom. It is not a growth by accretion, as in crystallization, but by intussusception, as in life. These ghostly things exhibit the phenomena of circulation and respiration and nutrition, and a crude sort of reproduction by budding; they repair their injuries, and are able to perform periodic movements, just as does an animal or a plant; they have a period of vigorous youthful growth, of old age, of decay, and of death. In form, in color, in texture, and in cell structure, they imitate so closely the cell structures of organic growth as to suggest something uncanny or diabolical. And yet the author of them does not claim that they are alive. They are not edible, they contain no protoplasm - no starch or sugar or peptone or fats or carbohydrates. These chemical creations by Dr. Leduc are still dead matter - dead colloids - only one remove from crystallization; on the road to life, fore-runners of life, but not life. If he could set up the chlorophyllian process in his chemical reactions among inorganic compounds, the secret of life would be in his hands. But only the green leaf can

John Burroughs

produce chlorophyll; and yet, which was first, the leaf or the chlorophyll?

Professor Czapek is convinced that "some substances must exist in protoplasm which are directly responsible for the life processes," and yet the chemists cannot isolate and identify those substances.

How utterly unmechanical a living body is, at least how far it transcends mere mechanics is shown by what the chemists call "autolysis." Pulverize your watch, and you have completely destroyed everything that made it a watch except the dead matter; but pulverize or reduce to a pulp a living plant, and though you have destroyed all cell structure, you have not yet destroyed the living substance; you have annihilated the mechanism, but you have not killed the something that keeps up the life process. Protoplasm takes time to die, but your machine stops instantly, and its elements are no more potent in a new machine than they were at first. "In the pulp prepared by grinding down living organisms in a mortar, some vital phenomena continue for a long time." The life processes cease, and the substances or elements of the dead body remain as before. Their chemical reactions are the same. There is no new chemistry, no new mechanics, no new substance in a live body, but there is a new tendency or force or impulse acting in matter, inspiring it, so to speak, to new ends. It is here that idealism parts company with exact science. It is here that the philosophers go one way, and the rigid scientists the other. It is from this point of view that the philosophy of Henri Bergson, based so largely as it is upon scientific material, has been so bitterly assailed from the scientific camp.

The living cell is a wonderful machine, but if we ask which is first, life or the cell, where are we? There is the synthetical reaction in the cell, and the analytical or splitting reaction - the organizing, and the disorganizing processes - what keeps up this seesaw and preserves the equilibrium? A life force, said the older scientists; only chemical laws, say the new. A prodigious change in the behavior of matter is wrought by life, and whether we say it is by chemical laws, or by a life force, the mystery remains.

The whole secret of life centres in the cell, in the plant cell; and this cell does not exceed .005 millimetres in diameter. An enormous number of chemical reactions take place in this minute space. It is a world in little. Here are bodies of different shapes whose service is to absorb carbon dioxide, and form sugar and carbohydrates. Must we go outside of matter itself, and of chemical reactions, to account for it? Call this unknown factor "vital force," as has so long been done, or name it "biotic energy," as Professor Moore has lately done, and the mystery remains the same. It is a new behavior in matter, call it by what name we will.

Inanimate nature seems governed by definite laws; that is, given the same conditions, the same results always follow. The reactions between two chemical elements under the same conditions are always the same. The physical forces go their unchanging ways, and are variable only as the conditions vary. In dealing with them we know exactly what to expect. We know at what degree of temperature, under the same conditions, water will boil, and at what degree of temperature it will freeze. Chance and probability play no part in such matters. But when we reach the world of animate nature, what a contrast we behold! Here, within certain limits, all is in perpetual flux and change. Living bodies are never two moments the same. Variability is the rule. We never know just how a living body will behave, under given conditions, till we try it. A late spring frost may kill nearly every bean stalk or potato plant or hill of corn in your garden, or nearly every shoot upon your grapevine. The survivors have greater powers of resistance - a larger measure of that mysterious something we call vitality. One horse will endure hardships and exposures that will kill scores of others. What will agitate one community will not in the same measure agitate another. What will break or discourage one human heart will sit much more lightly upon another. Life introduces an element of uncertainty or indeterminateness that we do not find in the inorganic world.

Bodies still have their laws or conditions of activity, but they are elastic and variable. Among living things we have in a measure escaped from the iron necessity that holds the world of dead matter in its grip. Dead matter ever tends to a static equilibrium; living matter to a dynamic poise, or a balance between the intake and the output of energy. Life is a peculiar activity in matter. If the bicyclist stops, his wheel falls down; no mechanical contrivance could be devised that could take his place on the wheel, and no combination of purely chemical and physical forces can alone do with matter what life does with it. The analogy here hinted at is only tentative. I would not imply that the relation of life to matter is merely mechanical and external, like that of the rider to his wheel. In life, the rider and his wheel are one, but when life vanishes, the wheel falls down. The chemical and physical activity of matter is perpetual; with a high-power microscope we may see the Brunonian movement in liquids and gases any time and at all times, but the movement we call vitality dominates these and turns them to new ends. I suppose the nature of the activity of the bombarding molecules of gases and liquids is the same in our bodies as out; that turmoil of the particles goes on forever; it is, in itself, blind, fateful, purposeless; but life furnishes, or *is*, an organizing principle that brings order and purpose out of this chaos. It does not annul any of the mechanical or chemical principles, but under its tutelage or inspiration they produce a host of new substances, and a world of new and beautiful and wonderful forms.

IV

Bergson says the intellect is characterized by a natural inability to understand life. Certain it is, I think, that science alone cannot grasp its mystery. We must finally appeal to philosophy; we must have recourse to ideal values - to a non-scientific or super-scientific principle. We cannot live intellectually or emotionally upon science alone. Science reveals to us the relations and inter-dependence of things in the physical world and their relations to our physical well-being; philosophy reveals their relations to our mental and spiritual life, their meanings and their ideal values. Poor, indeed, is the man who has no philosophy, no commanding outlook over the tangles and contradictions of the world of sense. There is probably some unknown and unknowable factor involved in the genesis of life, but that that factor or principle does not belong to the natural, universal order is unthinkable. Yet to fail to see that what we must call intelligence pervades and is active in all organic nature is to be spiritually blind. But to see it as something foreign to or separable from nature is to do violence to our faith in the constancy and sufficiency of the natural order. One star differeth from another in glory. There are degrees of mystery in the universe. The most mystifying thing in inorganic nature is electricity, - that disembodied energy that slumbers in the ultimate particles of matter, unseen, unfelt, unknown, till it suddenly leaps forth with such terrible vividness and power on the face of the storm, or till we summon it through the transformation of some other form of energy. A still higher and more inscrutable mystery is life, that something which clothes itself in each infinitely varied and beautiful as well as unbeautiful form of matter. We can evoke electricity at will from many different sources, but we can evoke life only from other life; the biogenetic law is inviolable.

Professor Soddy says, "Natural philosophy may explain a rainbow but not a rabbit." There is no secret about a rainbow; we can produce it at will out of perfectly colorless beginnings.

"But nothing but rabbits will or can produce a rabbit, a proof again that we cannot say what a rabbit is, though we may have a perfect knowledge of every anatomical and microscopic detail."

To regard life as of non-natural origin puts it beyond the sphere of legitimate inquiry; to look upon it as of natural origin, or as bound in a chain of chemical sequences, as so many late biochemists do, is still to put it where our science cannot unlock the mystery. If we should ever succeed in producing living matter in our laboratories, it would not lessen the mystery any more than the birth of a baby in the household lessens the mystery of generation. It only brings it nearer home.

V

What is peculiar to organic nature is the living cell. Inside the cell, doubtless, the same old chemistry and physics go on - the same universal law of the transformation of energy is operative. In its minute compass the transmutation of the inorganic into the organic, which constitutes what Tyndall called "the miracle and the mystery of vitality," is perpetually enacted. But what is the secret of the cell itself? Science is powerless to tell us. You may point out to your heart's content that only chemical and physical forces are discoverable in living matter; that there is no element or force in a plant that is not in the stone beside which it grew, or in the soil in which it takes root; and yet, until your chemistry and your physics will enable you to produce the living cell, or account for its mysterious self-directed activities, your science avails not. "Living cells," says a late European authority, "possess most effective means to accelerate reactions and to cause surprising chemical results."

Behold the four principal elements forming stones and soils and water and air for whole geologic or astronomic ages, and then behold them forming plants and animals, and finally forming the brains that give us art and literature and philosophy and modern civilization. What prompted the elements to this new and extraordinary behavior? Science is dumb before such a question.

Living bodies are immersed in physical conditions as in a sea. External agencies - light, moisture, air, gravity, mechanical and chemical influences - cause great changes in them; but their power to adapt themselves to these changes, and profit by them, remains unexplained. Are morphological processes identical with chemical ones?

In the inorganic world we everywhere see mechanical adjustment, repose, stability, equilibrium, through the action and interaction of outward physical forces; a natural bridge is a striking example of the action of blind mechanical forces among the rocks. In the organic world we see living adaptation which involves a non-mechanical principle. An adjustment is an outward fitting together of parts; an adaptation implies something flowing, unstable, plastic, compromising; it is a moulding process; passivity on one side, and activity on the other. Living things struggle; they struggle up as well as down; they struggle all round the circle, while the pull of dead matter is down only.

Behold what a good chemist a plant is! With what skill it analyzes the carbonic acid in the air, retaining the carbon and returning the oxygen to the atmosphere! Then the plant can do what no chemist has yet been able to do; it can manufacture chlorophyll, a substance which is the basis of all life on the globe. Without chlorophyll (the green substance in plants) the solar energy could not be stored up in the vegetable world. Chlorophyll makes the plant, and the plant makes chlorophyll. To ask which is first is to call up the old puzzle, Which is first, the egg, or the hen that laid it?

According to Professor Soddy, the engineer's unit of power, that of the British cart-horse, has to be multiplied many times in a machine before it can do the work of a horse. He says that a car which two horses used to pull, it now takes twelve or fifteen engine-horse to pull. The machine horse belongs to a different order. He does not respond to the whip; he has no nervous system; he has none of the mysterious reserve power which a machine built up of living cells seems to possess; he is inelastic, non-creative, non-adaptive; he cannot take advantage of the ground; his pull is a dead, unvarying pull. Living energy is elastic, adaptive, self-directive, and suffers little loss through friction, or through imperfect adjustment of the parts. A live body converts its fuel into energy at a low temperature. One of the great problems of the mechanics of the future is to develop electricity or power directly from fuel and thus cut out the enormous loss of eighty or ninety per cent which we now suffer. The growing body does this all the time; life possesses this secret; the solar energy stored up in fuel suffers no loss in being transformed into work by the animal mechanism.

Soddy asks whether or not the minute cells of the body may not have the power of taking advantage of the difference in temperature of the molecules bombarding them, and thus of utilizing energy that is beyond the capacity of the machinery of the motor-car. Man can make no machine that can avail itself of the stores of energy in the uniform temperature of the earth or air or water, or that can draw upon the potential energy of the atoms, but it may be that the living cell can do this, and thus a horse can pull more than a one-horse-power engine. Soddy makes the suggestive inquiry: "If life begins in a single cell, does intelligence? does the physical distinction between living and dead matter begin in the jostling molecular crowd? Inanimate molecules, in all their movements, obey the law of probability, the law which governs the successive falls of a true die. In the presence of a rudimentary intelligence, do they still follow that law, or do they now obey another law - the law of a die that is loaded?" In a machine the energy of fuel has first to be converted into heat before it is available, but in a living machine the chemical energy of food undergoes direct transformation into work, and the wasteful heat-process is cut off.

VI

Professor Soddy, in discussing the relation of life to energy, does not commit himself to the theory of the vitalistic or non-mechanical origin of life, but makes the significant statement that there is a consensus of opinion that the life processes are not bound by the second law of thermo-dynamics, namely, the law of the non-availability of the energy latent in low temperatures, or in the chaotic movements of molecules everywhere around us. To get energy, one must have a fall or an incline of some sort, as of water from a higher to a lower level, or of temperature from a higher to a lower degree, or of electricity from one condition of high stress to another less so. But the living machine seems able to dispense with this break or incline, or else has the secret of creating one for itself.

In the living body the chemical energy of food is directly transformed into work, without first being converted into heat. Why a horse can do more work than a one-horse-power engine is probably because his living cells can and do draw upon this molecular energy. Molecules of matter outside the living body all obey the law of probability, or the law of chance; but inside the living body they at least seem to obey some other law - the law of design, or of dice that are loaded, as Soddy says. They are more likely always to act in a particular way. Life supplies a directing agency. Soddy asks if the physical distinction between living and dead matter begins in the jostling molecular crowd - begins by the crowd being directed and governed in a particular way. If so, by what? Ah! that is the question. Science will have none of it, because science would have to go outside of matter for such an agent, and that science cannot do. Such a theory implies intelligence apart from matter, or working in matter. Is that a hard proposition? Intelligence clearly works in our bodies and brains, and in those of all the animals - a controlled and directed activity in matter that seems to be life. The cell which builds up all living bodies behaves not like a machine, but like a living being; its activities, so far as we can judge, are spontaneous, its motions and all its other processes are self-prompted. But, of course, in it the mechanical, the chemical, and the vital are so blended, so interdependent, that we may never hope to separate them; but without the activity called vital, there would be no cell, and hence no body.

It were unreasonable to expect that scientific analysis should show that the physics and chemistry of a living body differs from that of the non-living. What is new and beyond the reach of science to explain is the *kind of activity* of these elements. They enter into new compounds; they build up bodies that have new powers and properties; they people the seas and the air and the earth with living creatures, they build the body and brain of man. The secret of the activity in matter that we call vital is certainly beyond the power of science to tell us. It is like expecting that the paint and oil used in a great picture must differ from those in a daub. The great artist mixed his paint with brains, and the universal elements in a living body are mixed with something that science cannot disclose. Organic chemistry does not differ intrinsically from inorganic; the difference between the two lies in the purposive activity of the elements that build up a living body.

Or is life, as a New England college professor claims, "an *x*-entity, additional to matter and energy, but of the same cosmic rank as they," and "manifesting itself to our senses only through its power to keep a certain quantity of matter and energy in the continuous orderly ferment we call life"?

I recall that Huxley said that there was a third reality in this universe besides matter and energy, and this third reality was consciousness. But neither the "*x*-entity" of Professor Ganong nor the "consciousness" of Huxley can be said to be of the same cosmic rank as matter and energy, because they do not pervade the universe as matter and energy do. These forces abound throughout all space and endure throughout all time, but life and consciousness are flitting and uncertain pheno-mena of matter. A prick of a pin, or a blow from a hammer, may destroy both. Unless we consider them as potential in all matter (and who shall say that they are not?) may we look upon them as of cosmic rank?

It is often urged that it is not the eye that sees, or the brain that thinks, but something in them. But it is something in them that never went into them; it arose in them. It is the living eye and the living brain that do the seeing and the thinking. When the life activity ceases, these organs cease to see and to think. Their activity is kept up by certain physiological processes in the organs of the body, and to ask what keeps up these is like the puppy trying to overtake its own tail, or to run a race with its own shadow.

The brain is not merely the organ of the mind in an external and mechanical sense; it is the mind. When we come to living things, all such analogies fail us. Life is not a thing; thought is not a thing; but rather the effect of a certain activity in matter, which mind alone can recognize. When we try to explain or account for that which we are, it is as if a man were trying to lift himself.

Life seems like something apart. It does not seem to be amenable to the law of the correlation and conservation of forces. You cannot transform it into heat or light or electricity. The force which a man extracts from the food he eats while he is writing a poem, or doing any other mental work, seems lost to the universe. The force which the engine, or any machine, uses up, reappears as work done, or as heat or light or some other physical manifestation. But the energy of foodstuffs which a man uses up in a mental effort does not appear again in the circuit of the law of the conservation of energy. A man uses up more energy in his waking moments, though his body be passive, than in his sleeping. What we call mental force cannot be accounted for in terms of physical force. The sun's energy goes into our bodies through the food we eat, and so runs our mental faculties, but how does it get back again into the physical realm? Science does not know.

It must be some sort of energy that lights the lamps of the

firefly and the glow-worm, and it must be some sort or degree of energy that keeps consciousness going. The brain of a Newton, or of a Plato, must make a larger draft on the solar energy latent in food-stuffs than the brain of a day laborer, and his body less. The same amount of food-consumption, or of oxidation, results in physical force in the one case, and mental force in the other, but the mental force escapes the great law of the equivalence of the material forces.

John Fiske solves the problem when he drops his physical science and takes up his philosophy, declaring that the relation of the mind to the body is that of a musician to his instrument, and this is practically the position of Sir Oliver Lodge.

Inheritance and adaptation, says Haeckel, are sufficient to account for all the variety of animal and vegetable forms on the earth. But is there not a previous question? Do we not want inheritance and adaptation accounted for? What mysteries they hold! Does the river-bed account for the river? How can a body adapt itself to its environment unless it possess an inherent, plastic, changing, and adaptive principle? A stone does not adapt itself to its surroundings; its change is external and not internal. There is mechanical adjustment between inert bodies, but there is no adaptation without the push of life. A response to new conditions by change of form implies something actively responsive - something that profits by the change.

VII

If we could tell what determines the division of labor in the hive of bees or a colony of ants, we could tell what determines the division of labor among the cells in the body. A hive of bees and a colony of ants is a unit - a single organism. The spirit of the body, that which regulates all its economies, which directs all its functions, which cooordinates its powers, which brings about all its adaptations, which adjusts it to its environment, which sees to its repairs, heals its wounds, meets its demands, provides more force when more is needed, which makes one organ help do the work of another, which wages war on disease germs by specific ferments, which renders us immune to this or that disease; in fact, which carries on all the processes of our physical life without asking leave or seeking counsel of us, - all this is on another plane from the mechanical or chemical - super-mechanical.

The human spirit, the brute spirit, the vegetable spirit - all are mere names to fill a void. The spirit of the oak, the beech, the pine, the palm - how different! how different the plan or idea or interior economies of each, though the chemical and mechanical processes are the same, the same mineral and gaseous elements build them up, the same sun is their architect! But what physical principle can account for the difference between a pine and an oak, or, for that matter, between a man and his dog, or a bird and a fish, or a crow and a lark? What play and action or interaction and reaction of purely chemical and mechanical forces can throw any light on the course evolution has taken in the animal life of the globe - why the camel is the camel, and the horse the horse? or in the development of the nervous system, or the circulatory system, or the digestive system, or of the eye, or of the ear?

A living body is never in a state of chemical repose, but inorganic bodies usually are. Take away the organism and the environment remains essentially the same; take away the environment and the organism changes rapidly and perishes -

it goes back to the inorganic. Now, what keeps up the constant interchange - this seesaw? The environment is permanent; the organism is transient. The spray of the falls is permanent; the bow comes and goes. Life struggles to appropriate the environment; a rock, for example, does not, in the same sense, struggle with its surroundings, it weathers passively, but a tree struggles with the winds, and to appropriate minerals and water from the soil, and the leaves struggle to store up the sun's energy. The body struggles to eliminate poisons or to neutralize them; it becomes immune to certain diseases, learns to resist them; the thing is *alive*. Organisms struggle with one another; inert bodies clash and pulverize one another, but do not devour one another.

Life is a struggle between two forces, a force within and a force without, but the force within does all the struggling. The air does not struggle to get into the lungs, nor the lime and iron to get into our blood. The body struggles to digest and assimilate the food; the chlorophyll in the leaf struggles to store up the solar energy. The environment is unaware of the organism; the light is indifferent to the sensitized plate of the photographer. Something in the seed we plant avails itself of the heat and the moisture. The relation is not that of a thermometer or hygrometer to the warmth and moisture of the air; it is a vital relation.

Life may be called an aquatic phenomenon, because there can be no life without water. It may be called a thermal phenomenon, because there can be no life below or above a certain degree of temperature. It may be called a chemical phenomenon, because there can be no life without chemical reactions. Yet none of these things define life. We may discuss biological facts in terms of chemistry without throwing any light on the nature of life itself. If we say the particular essence of life is chemical, do we mean any more than that life is inseparable from chemical reactions?

After we have mastered the chemistry of life, laid bare all its processes, named all its transformations and transmutations, analyzed the living cell, seen the inorganic pass into the organic, and beheld chemical reaction, the chief priestess of this hidden rite, we shall have to ask ourselves, Is chemistry the creator of life, or does life create or use chemistry? These "chemical reaction complexes" in living cells, as the biochemists call them, are they the cause of life, or only the effect of life? We shall decide according to our temperaments or our habits of thought.

IX

THE JOURNEYING ATOMS

I

Emerson confessed in his "Journal" that he could not read the physicists; their works did not appeal to him. He was probably repelled by their formulas and their mathematics. But add a touch of chemistry, and he was interested. Chemistry leads up to life. He said he did not think he would feel threatened or insulted if a chemist should take his protoplasm, or mix his hydrogen, oxygen, and carbon, and make an animalcule incontestably swimming and jumping before his eyes. It would be only evidence of a new degree of power over matter which man had attained to. It would all finally redound to the glory of matter itself, which, it appears, "is impregnated with thought and heaven, and is really of God, and not of the Devil, as we had too hastily believed." This conception of matter underlies the new materialism of such men as Huxley and Tyndall. But there is much in the new physics apart from its chemical aspects that ought to appeal to the Emersonian type of mind. Did not Emerson in his first poem, "The Sphinx," sing of

> Journeying atoms,
> Primordial wholes?

In those ever-moving and indivisible atoms he touches the very corner-stone of the modern scientific conception of matter. It is hardly an exaggeration to say that in this conception we are brought into contact with a kind of transcendental physics. A new world for the imagination is open - a world where the laws and necessities of ponderable bodies do not apply. The world of gross matter disappears, and in its place we see matter dematerialized, and escaping from the bondage of the world of tangible bodies; we see a world where friction is abolished, where perpetual motion is no longer impossible; where two bodies may occupy the same space at the same time; where collisions and disruptions take place without loss of energy; where subtraction often means more - as when the poison of a substance is rendered more virulent by the removal of one or more atoms of one of the elements; and where addition often means less - as when three parts of the gases of oxygen and hydrogen unite and form only two parts of watery vapor; where mass and form, centre and circumference, size and structure, exist without any of the qualities ordinarily associated with these things through our experience in a three-dimension world. We see, or contemplate, bodies which are indivisible; if we divide them, their nature changes; if we divide a molecule of water, we get atoms of hydrogen and oxygen gas; if we divide a molecule of salt, we get atoms of chlorine gas and atoms of the metal sodium, which means that we have reached a point where matter is no longer divisible in a mechanical sense, but only in a chemical sense; which again means that great and small, place and time, inside and outside, dimensions and spatial relations, have lost their ordinary meanings. Two bodies get inside of each other. To the physicist, heat and motion are one; light is only a mechanical vibration in the ether; sound is only a vibration in the air, which the ear interprets as sound. The world is as still as death till the living ear comes to receive the vibrations in the air; motion, or the energy which it implies, is the life of the universe.

Physics proves to us the impossibility of perpetual motion among visible, tangible bodies, at the same time that it reveals to us a world where perpetual motion is the rule - the world of molecules and atoms. In the world of gross matter, or of ponderable bodies, perpetual motion is impossible because here it takes energy, or its equivalent, to beget energy. Friction very soon turns the kinetic energy of motion into the potential energy of heat, which quickly disappears in that great sea of energy, the low uniform temperature of the earth. But when we reach the interior world of matter, the world of molecules, atoms, and electrons, we have reached a world where perpetual motion *is* the rule; we have reached the fountain-head of energy, and the motion of one body is not at the expense of the motion of some other body, but is a part of the spontaneous struggling and jostling and vibration that go on forever in all the matter of the universe. What is called the Brunonian movement (first discovered by the botanist Robert Brown in 1827) is within reach of the eye armed with a high-power microscope. Look into any liquid that holds in suspension very small particles of solid matter, such as dust particles in the air, or the granules of ordinary water-color paints dissolved in water: not a single one of the particles is at rest; they are all mysteriously agitated; they jump hither and thither; it is a wild chaotic whirl and dance of minute particles. Brown at first thought they were alive, but they were only non-living particles dancing to the same tune which probably sets suns and systems whirling in the heavens. Ramsay says that tobacco smoke confined in the small flat chamber formed in the slide of a microscope, shows this movement, in appearance like the flight of minute butterflies. The Brunonian movement is now believed to be due to the bombardment of the particles by the molecules of the liquid or gas in which they are suspended. The smaller the particles, the livelier they are. These particles themselves are made up of a vast number of molecules, among which the same movement or agitation, much more intense, is supposed to be taking place; the atoms which compose the molecules are dancing and frisking about like gnats in the air, and the electrons inside the atoms are still more rapidly changing places.

We meet with the same staggering figures in the science of the infinitely little that we do in the science of the infinitely vast.

Thus the physicist deals with a quantity of matter a million million times smaller than can be detected in the most delicate chemical balance. Molecules inconceivably small rush about in molecular space inconceivably small. Ramsay calculates how many collisions the molecules of gas make with other molecules every second, which is four and one half quintillions. This staggers the mind like the tremendous revelations of astronomy. Mathematics has no trouble to compute the figures, but our slow, clumsy minds feel helpless before them. In every drop of water we drink, and in every mouthful of air we breathe, there is a movement and collision of particles so rapid in every second of time that it can only be expressed by four with eighteen naughts. If the movement of these particles were attended by friction, or if the energy of their impact were translated into heat, what hot mouthfuls we should have! But the heat, as well as the particles, is infinitesimal, and is not perceptible.

II

The molecules and atoms and electrons into which science resolves matter are hypothetical bodies which no human eye has ever seen, or ever can see, but they build up the solid frame of the universe. The air and the rocks are not so far apart in their constituents as they might seem to our senses. The invisible and indivisible molecules of oxygen which we breathe, and which keep our life-currents going, form about half the crust of the earth. The soft breeze that fans and refreshes us, and the rocks that crush us, are at least half-brothers. And herein we get a glimpse of the magic of chemical combinations. That mysterious property in matter which we call chemical affinity, a property beside which human affinities and passions are tame and inconstant affairs, is the architect of the universe. Certain elements attract certain other elements with a fierce and unalterable attraction, and when they unite, the resultant compound is a body totally unlike either of the constituents. Both substances have disappeared, and a new one has taken their place. This is the magic of chemical change. A physical change, as of water into ice, or into steam, is a simple matter; it is merely a matter of more or less heat; but the change of oxygen and hydrogen into water, or of chlorine gas and the mineral sodium into common salt, is a chemical change. In nature, chlorine and sodium are not found in a free or separate state; they hunted each other up long ago, and united to produce the enormous quantities of rock salt that the earth holds. One can give his imagination free range in trying to picture what takes place when two or more elements unite chemically, but probably there is no physical image that can afford even a hint of it. A snake trying to swallow himself, or two fishes swallowing each other, or two bullets meeting in the air and each going through the centre of the other, or the fourth dimension, or almost any other impossible thing, from the point of view of tangible bodies, will serve as well as anything. The atoms seem to get inside of one another, to jump down one another's throats, and to suffer a complete transformation. Yet we know that they do not; oxygen is still oxygen, and carbon still carbon, amid all the strange partnerships entered into, and all the disguises assumed. We can easily evoke hydrogen and oxygen from water, but just how their molecules unite, how they interpenetrate and are lost in one another, it is impossible for us to conceive.

We cannot visualize a chemical combination because we have no experience upon which to found it. It is so fundamentally unlike a mechanical mixture that even our imagination can give us no clew to it. It is thinkable that the particles of two or more substances however fine, mechanically mixed, could be seen and recognized if sufficiently magnified; but in a chemical combination, say like iron sulphide, no amount of magnification could reveal the two elements of iron and sulphur. They no longer exist. A third substance unlike either has taken their place.

We extract aluminum from clay, but no conceivable power of vision could reveal to us that metal in the clay. It is there only potentially. In a chemical combination the different substances interpenetrate and are lost in one another: they are not mechanically separable nor individually distinguishable. The iron in the red corpuscles of the blood is not the metal we know, but one of its many chemical disguises. Indeed it seems as if what we call the ultimate particles of matter did not belong to the visible order and hence were incapable of magnification.

That mysterious force, chemical affinity, is the true and original magic. That two substances should cleave to each other and absorb each other and produce a third totally unlike either is one of the profound mysteries of science. Of the nature of the change that takes place, I say, we can form no image. Chemical force is selective; it is not promiscuous and indiscriminate like gravity, but specific and individual. Nearly all the elements have their preferences and they will choose no other. Oxygen comes the nearest to being a free lover among the elements, but its power of choice is limited.

Science conceives of all matter as grained or discrete, like a bag of shot, or a pile of sand. Matter does not occupy space continuously, not even in the hardest substances, such as the diamond; there is space, molecular space, between the particles. A rifle bullet whizzing past is no more a continuous body than is a flock of birds wheeling and swooping in the air. Air spaces separate the birds, and molecular spaces separate the molecules of the bullet. Of course it is unthinkable that indivisible particles of matter can occupy space and have dimensions. But science goes upon this hypothesis, and the hypothesis proves itself.

After we have reached the point of the utmost divisibility of matter in the atom, we are called upon to go still further and divide the indivisible. The electrons, of which the atom is composed, are one hundred thousand times smaller, and two thousand times lighter than the smallest particle hitherto recognized, namely, the hydrogen atom. A French physicist conceives of the electrons as rushing about in the interior of the atom like swarms of gnats whirling about in the dome of a cathedral. The smallest particle of dust that we can recognize in the air is millions of times larger than the atom, and millions of millions of times larger than the electron. Yet science avers that the manifestations of energy which we call light, radiant heat, magnetism, and electricity, all come from the activities of the electrons. Sir J. J. Thomson conceives of a free electron as dashing about from one atom to another at a speed so great as to change its location forty million times a second. In the electron we have matter dematerialized; the electron is not a material particle. Hence the step to the electric constitution of matter is an easy one. In the last analysis we have pure disembodied energy. "With many of the feelings of an air-man," says Soddy, "who has left behind for the first time the solid ground beneath him," we make this plunge into the demonstrable verities of the newest physics; matter in the old sense - gross matter - fades away. To the three states in which we have always known it, the solid, the liquid, and the gaseous, we must add a fourth, the ethereal - the state of matter which Sir Oliver Lodge thinks borders on, or is identical with, what we call the spiritual, and which affords the key to all the occult phenomena of life and mind.

As we have said, no human eye has ever seen, or will see, an atom; only the mind's eye, or the imagination, sees atoms and molecules, yet the atomic theory of matter rests upon the sure foundation of experimental science. Both the chemist and the physicist are as convinced of the existence of these atoms as they are of the objects we see and touch. The theory "is a necessity to explain the experimental facts of chemical composition." "Through metaphysics first," says Soddy, "then through alchemy and chemistry, through physical and astronomical spectroscopy, lastly through radio-activity, science has slowly groped its way to the atom." The physicists make definite statements about these hypothetical bodies all based upon definite chemical phenomena. Thus Clerk Maxwell assumes that they are spherical, that the spheres are hard and elastic like billiard-balls, that they collide and glance off from one another in the same way, that is, that they collide at their surfaces and not at their centres.

Only two of our senses make us acquainted with matter in a state which may be said to approach the atomic - smell and taste. Odors are material emanations, and represent a division of matter into inconceivably small particles. What are the perfumes we smell but emanations, flying atoms or electrons, radiating in all directions, and continuing for a shorter or longer time without any appreciable diminution in bulk or weight of the substances that give them off? How many millions or trillions of times does the rose divide its heart in the perfume it sheds so freely upon the air? The odor of the musk of certain animals lingers under certain conditions for years. The imagination is baffled in trying to conceive of the number and minuteness of the particles which the fox leaves of itself in the snow where its foot was imprinted - so palpable that the scent of a hound can seize upon them hours after the fox has passed! The all but infinite divisibility of matter is proved by every odor that the breeze brings us from field and wood, and by the delicate flavors that the tongue detects in the food we eat and drink. But these emanations and solutions that affect our senses probably do not represent a chemical division of matter; when we smell an apple or a flower, we probably get a real fragment of the apple, or of the flower, and not one or more of its chemical constituents represented by atoms or electrons. A chemical analysis of odors, if it were possible, would probably show the elements in the same state of combination as the substances from which the odors emanated.

The physicists herd these ultimate particles of matter about; they have a regular circus with them; they make them go through films and screens; they guide them through openings; they count them as their tiny flash is seen on a sensitized plate; they weigh them; they reckon their velocity. The alpha-rays from radio-active substances are swarms of tiny meteors flying at the incredible speed of twelve thousand miles a second, while the meteors of the midnight sky fly at the speed of only forty miles a second. Those alpha particles are helium atoms. They are much larger than beta particles, and have less penetrative power. Sir J. J. Thomson has devised a method by which he has been able to photograph the atoms. The photographic plate upon which their flight is recorded suggests a shower of shooting stars. Oxygen is found to be made up of atoms of several different forms.

III

The "free path" of molecules, both in liquids and in gases, is so minute as to be beyond the reach of the most powerful microscope. This free path in liquids is a zigzag course, owing to the perpetual collisions with other molecules. The molecular behavior of liquids differs from that of gases only in what is called surface tension. Liquids have a skin, a peculiar stress of the surface molecules; gases do not, but tend to dissipate and fill all space. A drop of water remains intact till vaporization sets in; then it too becomes more and more diffused.

When two substances combine chemically, more or less heat is evolved. When the combination is effected slowly, as in an animal's body, heat is slowly evolved. When the combustion is rapid, as in actual fire, heat is rapidly evolved. The same phenomenon may reach the eye as light, and the hand as heat, though different senses get two different impressions of the same thing. So a mechanical disturbance may reach the ear as sound, and be so interpreted, and reach the hand as motion in matter. In combustion, the oxygen combines rapidly with the carbon, giving out heat and light and carbon dioxide, but why it does so admits of no explanation. Herein again is where life differs from fire; we can describe combustion in terms of chemistry, but after we have described life in the same terms something - and this something is the main thing - remains untouched.

The facts of radio-activity alone demonstrate the truth of the atomic theory. The beta rays, or emanations from radium, penetrating one foot of solid iron are very convincing. And this may go on for hundreds of years without any appreciable diminution of size or weight of the radio-active substance. "A gram of such substance," says Sir Oliver Lodge, "might lose a few thousand of atoms a second, and yet we could not detect the loss if we continued to weigh it for a century." The volatile essences of organic bodies which we detect in odors and flavors, are not potent like the radium emanations. We can confine them and control them, but we cannot control the rays of radio-active matter any more than we can confine a spirit. We can separate the three different kinds of rays - the alpha, the beta, and the gamma - by magnetic devices, but we cannot cork them up and isolate them, as we can musk and the attar of roses.

And these emanations are taking place more or less continuously all about us and we know it not. In fact, we are at all times subjected to a molecular bombardment of which we never dream; minute projectiles, indivisible points of matter, are shot out at us in the form of electrons from glowing metals, from lighted candles, and from other noiseless and unsuspected batteries at a speed of tens of thousands of miles a second, and we are none the wiser for it. Indeed, if we could see or feel or be made aware of it, in what a different world we should find ourselves! How many million-or billion-fold our sense of sight and touch would have to be increased to bring this about! We live in a world of collisions, disruptions, and hurtling missiles of which our senses give us not the slightest evidence, and it is well that they do not. There is a tremendous activity in the air we breathe, in the water we drink, in the food we eat, and in the soil we walk upon, which, if magnified till our senses could take it in, would probably drive us mad. It is in this interior world of molecular activity, this world of electric vibrations and oscillations, that the many transformations of energy take place. This is the hiding-place of the lightning, of the electrons which moulded together make the thunderbolt. What an underworld of mystery and power it is! In it slumbers all the might and menace of the storm, the power that rends the earth and shakes the heavens. With the mind's eye one can see the indivisible atoms giving up their electrons, see the invisible hosts, in numbers beyond the power of mathematics to compute, being summoned and marshalled by some mysterious commander and hurled in terrible fiery phalanxes across the battlefield of the storm.

The physicist describes the atom and talks about it as if it were "a tangible body which one could hold in his hand like a baseball." "An atom," Sir Oliver Lodge says, "consists of a globular mass of positive electricity with minute negative electrons embedded in it." He speaks of the spherical form of the atom, and of its outer surface, of its centre, and of its passing through other atoms, and of the electrons that revolve around its centre as planets around a sun. The electron, one hundred thousand times smaller than an atom, yet has surface, and that surface is a dimpled and corrugated sheet - like the cover of a mattress. What a flight of the scientific imagination is that!

The disproportion between the size of an atom and the size of an electron is vastly greater than that between the sun and the earth. Represent an atom, says Sir Oliver Lodge, by a church one hundred and sixty feet long, eighty feet broad, and forty feet high; the electrons are like gnats inside it. Yet on the electric theory of matter, electrons are all of the atom there is; there is no church, but only the gnats rushing about. We know of nothing so empty and hollow, so near a vacuum, as matter in this conception of it. Indeed, in the new physics, matter is only a hole in the ether. Hence the newspaper joke about the bank sliding down and leaving the woodchuck-hole sticking out, looks like pretty good physics. The electrons give matter its inertia, and give it the force we call cohesion, give it its toughness, its strength, and all its other properties. They make water wet, and the diamond hard. They are the fountain-head of the immense stores of the inter-atomic energy, which, if it could be tapped and controlled, would so easily do all the work of the world. But this we cannot do. "We are no m orecompetent," says Professor Soddy, "to make use of these supplies of atomic energy than a savage, ignorant of how to kindle a fire, could make use of a steam-engine." The natural rate of flow of this energy from its atomic sources we get as heat, and it suffices to keep life going upon this planet. It is the source of all the activity we see upon the globe. Its results, in the geologic ages, are stored up for us in coal and oil and natural gas, and, in our day, are available in the winds, the tides, and the waterfalls, and in electricity.

IV

The electric constitution of matter is quite beyond anything we can imagine. The atoms are little worlds by themselves, and the whole mystery of life and death is in their keeping. The whole difference in the types of mind and character among men is supposed to be in their keeping. The different qualities and properties of bodies are in their keeping. Whether an object is hot or cold to our senses, depends upon the character of their vibrations; whether it be sweet or sour, poisonous or innocuous to us, depends upon how the atoms select their partners in the whirl and dance of their activities. The hardness and brilliancy of the diamond is supposed to depend upon how the atoms of carbon unite and join hands.

I have heard the view expressed that all matter, as such, is dead matter, that the molecules of hydrogen, oxygen, carbon, nitrogen, iron, phosphorus, calcium, and so on, in a living body, are themselves no more alive than the same molecules in inorganic matter. Nearly nine tenths of a living body is water; is not this water the same as the water we get at the spring or the brook? is it any more alive? does water undergo any chemical change in the body? is it anything more than a solvent, than a current that carries the other elements to all parts of the body? There are any number of chemical changes or reactions in a living body, but are the atoms and molecules that are involved in such changes radically changed? Can oxygen be anything but oxygen, or carbon anything but carbon? Is what we call life the result of their various new combinations? Many modern biologists hold to this view. In this conception merely a change in the order of arrangement of the molecules of a substance - which follows which or which is joined to which - is fraught with consequences as great as the order in which the letters of the alphabet are arranged in words, or the words themselves are arranged in sentences. The change of one letter in a word often utterly changes the meaning of that word, and the changing of a word in the sentence may give expression to an entirely different idea.

John Burroughs

Reverse the letters in the word "God," and you get the name of our faithful friend the dog. Huxley and Tyndall both taught that it was the way that the ultimate particles of matter are compounded that makes the whole difference between a cabbage and an oak, or between a frog and a man. It is a hard proposition. We know with scientific certainty that the difference between a diamond and a piece of charcoal, or between a pearl and an oyster-shell, is the way that the particles of carbon in the one case, and of calcium carbide in the other, are arranged. We know with equal certainty that the difference between certain chemical bodies, like alcohol and ether, is the arrangement of their ultimate particles, since both have the same chemical formula. We do not spell acetic acid, alcohol, sugar, starch, animal fat, vegetable oils, glycerine, and the like, with the same letters; yet nature compounds them all of the same atoms of carbon, hydrogen, and oxygen, but in different proportions and in different orders.

Chemistry is all-potent. A mechanical mixture of two or more elements is a simple affair, but a chemical mixture introduces an element of magic. No conjurer's trick can approach such a transformation as that of oxygen and hydrogen gases into water. The miracle of turning water into wine is tame by comparison. Dip plain cotton into a mixture of nitric and sulphuric acids and let it dry, and we have that terrible explosive, guncotton. Or, take the cellulose of which cotton is composed, and add two atoms of hydrogen and one of oxygen, and we have sugar. But we are to remember that the difference here indicated is not a quantitative, but a qualitative one, not one affecting bulk, but affecting structure. Truly chemistry works wonders. Take ethyl alcohol, or ordinary spirits of wine, and add four more atoms of carbon to the carbon molecule, and we have the poison carbolic acid. Pure alcohol can be turned into a deadly poison, not by adding to, but simply by taking from it; take out one atom of carbon and two of hydrogen from the alcohol molecule, and we have the poison methyl alcohol. But we are to remember that the difference here indicated is not a quantitative, but a qualitative one, not one affecting bulk, but affecting structure.

In our atmosphere we have a mechanical mixture of nitrogen and oxygen, four parts of nitrogen to one of oxygen. By uniting the nitrogen and oxygen chemically (N_2O) we have nitrous oxide, laughing-gas. Ordinary starch is made up of three different elements - six parts of carbon, ten parts of hydrogen, and five parts of oxygen ($C_6H_{10}O_5$). Now if we add water to this compound, we have a simple mixture of starch and water, but if we bring about a chemical union with the elements of water (hydrogen and oxygen), we have grape sugar. This sugar is formed in green leaves by the agency of sunlight, and is the basis of all plant and animal food, and hence one of the most important things in nature.

Carbon is a solid, and is seen in its pure state in the diamond, the hardest body in nature and the most valued of all precious stones, but it enters largely into all living bodies and is an important constituent of all the food we eat. As a gas, united with the oxygen of the air, forming carbon dioxide, it was present at the beginning of life, and probably helped kindle the first vital spark. In the shape of wood and coal, it now warms us and makes the wheels of our material civilization go round. Diamond stuff, through the magic of chemistry, plays one of the principle roles in our physical life; we eat it, and are warmed and propelled by it, and cheered by it. Taken as carbonic acid gas into our lungs, it poisons us; taken into our stomachs, it stimulates us; dissolved in water, it disintegrates the rocks, eating out the carbonate of lime which they contain. It is one of the principal actors in the drama of organized matter.

V

We have a good illustration of the power of chemistry, and how closely it is dogging the footsteps of life, in the many organic compounds it has built up out of the elements, such as sugar, starch, indigo, camphor, rubber, and so forth, all of which used to be looked upon as impossible aside from life-processes. It is such progress as this that leads some men of science to believe that the creation of life itself is within the reach of chemistry. I do not believe that any occult or transcendental principle bars the way, but that some unknown and perhaps unknowable condition does, as mysterious and unrepeatable as that which separates our mental life from our physical. The transmutation of the physical into the psychical takes place, but the secret of it we do not know. It does not seem to fall within the law of the correlation and the conservation of energy.

Free or single atoms are very rare; they all quickly find their mates or partners. This eagerness of the elements to combine is one of the mysteries. If the world of visible matter were at one stroke resolved into its constituent atoms, it would practically disappear; we might smell it, or taste it, if we were left, but we could not see it, or feel it; the water would vanish, the solid ground would vanish - more than half of it into oxygen atoms, and the rest mainly into silicon atoms.

The atoms of different bodies are all alike, and presumably each holds the same amount of electric energy. One wonders, then, how the order in which they are arranged can affect them so widely as to produce bodies so unlike as, say, alcohol and ether. This brings before us again the mystery of chemical arrangement or combination, so different from anything we know among tangible bodies. It seems to imply that each atom has its own individuality. Mix up a lot of pebbles together, and the result would be hardly affected by the order of the arrangement, but mix up a lot of people, and the result would be greatly affected by the fact of who is elbowing who. It seems the same among the mysterious atoms, as if some complemented or stimulated those next them, or had an opposite effect. But can we think of the atoms in a chemical compound as being next one another, or merely in juxtaposition? Do we not rather have to think of them as identified with one another to an extent that has no parallel in the world of ponderable bodies? A kind of sympathy or affinity makes them one in a sense that we only see realized among living beings.

Chemical activity is the first step from physical activity to vital activity, but the last step is taken rarely - the other two are universal. Chemical changes involve the atom. What do vital changes involve? We do not know. We can easily bring about the chemical changes, but not so the vital changes. A chemical change destroys one or more substances and produces others totally unlike them; a vital change breaks up substances and builds up other bodies out of them; it results in new compounds that finally cover the earth with myriads of new and strange forms.

X

THE VITAL ORDER

I

The mechanistic theory of life - the theory that all living things can be explained and fully accounted for on purely physico-chemical principles - has many defenders in our day. The main aim of the foregoing chapters is to point out the inadequacy of this view. At the risk of wearying my reader I am going to collect under the above heading a few more considerations bearing on this point.

A thing that grows, that develops, cannot, except by very free use of language, be called a machine. We speak of the body as a machine, but we have to qualify it by prefixing the adjective living - the living machine, which takes it out of the mechanical order of things fabricated, contrived, built up from without, and puts it in the order we call vital, the order of things self-developed from within, the order of things autonomous, as contrasted with things automatic. All the mechanical principles are operative in the life processes, but they have been vitalized, not changed in any way but in the service of a new order of reality. The heart with its chambers and valves is a pump that forces the blood through the system, but a pump that works itself and does not depend upon pneumatic pressure - a pump in which vital energy takes the place of gravitational energy. The peristaltic movement in the intestines involves a mechanical principle, but it is set up by an inward stimulus, and not by outward force. It is these inward stimuli, which of course involve chemical reactions, that afford the motive power for all living bodies and that put the living in another order from the mechanical. The eye is an optical instrument, - a rather crude one, it is said, - but it cannot be separated from its function, as can a mere instrument - the eye sees as literally as the brain thinks. In breathing we unconsciously apply the principle of the bellows; it is a bellows again which works itself, but the function of which, in a very limited sense, we can inhibit and control. An artificial, or man-made, machine always implies an artificer, but the living machine is not made in any such sense; it grows, it arises out of the organizing principle that becomes active in matter under conditions that we only dimly understand, and that we cannot reproduce.

The vital and the mechanical cooeperate in all our bodily functions. Swallowing our food is a mechanical process, the digestion of it is a chemical process and the assimilation and elimination of it a vital process. Inhaling and exhaling the air is a mechanical process, the oxidation of the blood is a chemical process, and the renewal of the corpuscles is a vital process. Growth, assimilation, elimination, reproduction, metabolism, and secretion, are all vital processes which cannot be described in terms of physics and chemistry. All our bodily movements - lifting, striking, walking, running - are mechanical, but seeing, hearing, and tasting, are of another order. And that which controls, directs, cooordinates, and inhibits our activities belongs to a still higher order, the psychic. The world of thoughts and emotions within us, while dependent upon and interacting with the physical world without us, cannot be accounted for in terms of the physical world. A living thing is more than a machine, more than a chemical laboratory.

We can analyze the processes of a tree into their mechanical and chemical elements, but there is besides a kind of force there which we must call vital. The whole growth and development of the tree, its manner of branching and gripping the soil, its fixity of species, its individuality - all imply something that does not belong to the order of the inorganic, automatic forces. In the living animal how the psychic stands related to the physical or physiological and arises out of it, science cannot tell us, but the relation must be real; only philosophy can grapple with that question. To resolve the psychic and the vital into the mechanical and chemical and refuse to see any other factors at work is the essence of materialism.

II

Any contrivance which shows an interdependence of parts, that results in unity of action, is super-mechanical. The solar system may be regarded as a unit, but it has not the purposive unity of a living body. It is one only in the sense that its separate bodies are all made of one stuff, and obey the same laws and move together in the same direction, but a living body is a unit because all its parts are in the service of one purposive end. An army is a unit, a flock of gregarious birds, a colony of ants or bees, is a unit because the spirit and purpose of one is the spirit and purpose of all; the unity is psychological.

Only living bodies are adaptive. Adaptation, of course, has its physics or its chemistry, because it is a physical phenomenon; but there is no adaptation of a rock or a clay-bank to its environment; there is only mechanical and chemical adjustment. The influence of the environment may bring about chemical and physical changes in a non-living body, but they are not purposive as in a living body. The fat in the seeds of plants in northern countries is liquid and solid at a lower temperature than in tropical climates. Living organisms alone react in a formative or deformative way to external stimuli. In warm climates the fur of animals and the wool of sheep become thin and light. The colder the climate, the thicker these coverings. Such facts only show that in the matter of adaptation among living organisms, there is a factor at work other than chemistry and physics - not independent of them, but making a purposive use of them. Cut off the central shoot that leads the young spruce tree upwards, and one of the shoots from the whirl of lateral branches below it slowly rises up and takes the place of the lost leader. Here is an action not prompted by the environment, but by the morphological needs of the tree, and it illustrates how different is its unity from the unity of a mere machine. I am only aiming to point out that in all living things the material forces behave in a purposive way to a degree that cannot be affirmed of them in non-living, and that, therefore, they imply intelligence.

Evidently the cells in the body do not all have the same degree of life, - that is, the same degree of irritability. The bone cells and the hair cells, for instance, can hardly be so much alive - or so irritable - as the muscle cells; nor these as intensely alive as the nerve and brain cells. Does not a bird possess a higher degree of life than a mollusk, or a turtle? Is not a brook trout more alive than a mud-sucker? You can freeze the latter as stiff as an icicle and resuscitate it, but not the former. There is a scale of degrees in life as clearly as there is a scale of degrees in temperature. There is an endless gradation of sensibilities of the living cells, dependent probably upon the degree of differentiation of function. Anaesthetics dull or suspend this irritability. The more highly developed and complex the nervous system, the higher the degree of life, till we pass from mere physical life to psychic life. Science might trace this difference to cell structure, but what brings about the change in the character of the cell, or starts the cells to building a complex nervous system, is a question unanswerable to science. The biologist imagines this and that about the invisible or hypothetical molecular structure; he assigns different functions to the atoms; some are for endosmosis, others for contraction, others for conduction of stimuli. Intramolecular oxygen plays a part. Other names are given to the mystery - the micellar strings of Naegeli, the biophores of Weismann, the plastidules of Haeckel; they all presuppose millions of molecules peculiarly arranged in the protoplasm.

On purely mechanical and chemical principles Tyndall accounts for the growth from the germ of a tree. The germ would be quiet, but the solar light and heat disturb its dreams, break up its atomic equilibrium. The germ makes an "effort" to restore it (why does it make an effort?), which effort is necessarily defeated and incessantly renewed, and in the turmoil or "scrapping" between the germ and the solar forces, matter is gathered from the soil and from the air and built into the special form of a tree. Why not in the form of a cabbage, or a donkey, or a clam? If the forces are purely automatic, why not? Why should matter be gathered in at all in a mechanical struggle between inorganic elements? But these are not all inorganic; the seed is organic. Ah! that makes the difference! That accounts for the "effort." So we have to have the organic to start with, then the rest is easy. No doubt the molecules of the seed would remain in a quiescent state, if they were not disturbed by external influences, chemical and mechanical. But there is something latent or potential in that seed that is the opposite of the mechanical, namely, the vital, and in what that consists, and where it came from, is the mystery.

III

I fancy that the difficulty which an increasing number of persons find in accepting the mechanistic view of life, or evolution, - the view which Herbert Spencer built into such a ponderous system of philosophy, and which such men as Huxley, Tyndall, Gifford, Haeckel, Verworn, and others, have upheld and illustrated, - is temperamental rather than logical. The view is distasteful to a certain type of mind - the flexible, imaginative, artistic, and literary type - the type that loves to see itself reflected in nature or that reads its own thoughts and emotions into nature. In a few eminent examples the two types of mind to which I refer seem more or less blended. Sir Oliver Lodge is a case in point. Sir Oliver is an eminent physicist who in his conception of the totality of things is yet a thoroughgoing idealist and mystic. His solution of the problem of living things is extra-scientific. He sees in life a distinct transcendental principle, not involved in the constitution of matter, but independent of it, entering into it and using it for its own purposes.

Tyndall was another great scientist with an inborn idealistic strain in him. His famous, and to many minds disquieting, declaration, made in his Belfast address over thirty years ago, that in matter itself he saw the promise and the potency of all terrestrial life, stamps him as a scientific materialist. But his conception of matter, as "at bottom essentially mystical and transcendental," stamps him as also an idealist. The idealist in him speaks very eloquently in the passage which, in the same address, he puts into the mouth of Bishop Butler, in the latter's imaginary debate with Lucretius: "Your atoms," says the Bishop, "are individually without sensation, much more are they without intelligence. May I ask you, then, to try your hand upon this problem. Take your dead hydrogen atoms, your dead oxygen atoms, your dead carbon atoms, your dead nitrogen atoms, your dead phosphorus atoms, and all the other atoms, dead as grains of shot, of which the brain is formed. Imagine them separate and sensationless, observe them running together and forming all imaginable combinations. This, as a purely mechanical process, is *seeable* by the mind. But can you see or dream, or in any way imagine, how out of that mechanical art, and from these individually dead atoms, sensation, thought, and emotion are to arise? Are you likely to extract Homer out of the rattling of dice, or the Differential Calculus out of the clash of billiard balls?" Could any vitalist, or Bergsonian idealist have stated his case better?

Now the Bishop Butler type of mind - the visualizing, idealizing, analogy-loving, literary, and philosophical mind - is shared by a good many people; it is shared by or is characteristic of all the great poets, artists, seers, idealists of the world; it is the humanistic type that sees man everywhere reflected in nature; and is radically different from the strictly scientific type which dehumanizes nature and reduces it to impersonal laws and forces, which distrusts analogy and sentiment and poetry, and clings to a rigid logical method.

This type of mind is bound to have trouble in accepting the physico-chemical theory of the nature and origin of life. It visualizes life, sees it as a distinct force or principle working in and through matter but not of it, super-physical in its origin and psychological in its nature. This is the view Henri Bergson exploits in his "Creative Evolution." This is the view Kant took when he said, "It is quite certain that we cannot even satisfactorily understand, much less explain, the nature of an organism and its internal forces on purely mechanical principles." It is the view Goethe took when he said, "Matter can never exist without spirit, nor spirit without matter."

Tyndall says Goethe was helped by his poetic training in the field of natural history, but hindered as regards the physical and mechanical sciences. "He could not formulate distinct mechanical conceptions; he could not see the force of mechanical reasoning." His literary culture helped him to a literary interpretation of living nature, but not to a scientific explanation of it; it helped put him in sympathy with living things, and just to that extent barred him from the mechanistic

John Burroughs

conception of those of pure science. Goethe, like every great poet, saw the universe through the colored medium of his imagination, his emotional and aesthetic nature; in short, through his humanism, and not in the white light of the scientific reason. His contributions to literature were of the first order, but his contributions to science have not taken high rank. He was a "prophet of the soul," and not a disciple of the scientific understanding.

If we look upon life as inherent or potential in the constitution of matter, dependent upon outward physical and chemical conditions for its development, we are accounting for life in terms of matter and motion, and are in the ranks of the materialists. But if we find ourselves unable to set the ultimate particles of matter in action, or so working as to produce the reaction which results in life, without conceiving of some new force or principle operating upon them, then we are in the ranks of the vitalists or idealists. The idealists see the original atoms slumbering there in rock and sea and soil for untold ages, till, moved upon by some unknown factor, they draw together in certain fixed order and numbers, and life is the result. Something seems to put a spell upon them and cause them to behave so differently from the way they behaved before they were drawn into the life circuit.

When we think of life, as the materialists do, as of mechanico-chemical origin, or explicable in terms of the natural universal order, we think of the play of material forces amid which we live, we think of their subtle action and interaction all about us - of osmosis, capillarity, radio-activity, electricity, thermism, and the like; we think of the four states of matter, - solid, fluid, gaseous, and ethereal, - of how little our senses take in of their total activities, and we do not feel the need of invoking a transcendental principle to account for it.

Yet to fail to see that what we must call intelligence pervades and is active in all organic nature is to be spiritually blind. But to see it as something foreign to, or separable from, nature is to do violence to our faith in the constancy and sufficiency of the natural order. One star differeth from another star in glory. There are degrees of mystery in the universe. The most mysterious thing in inorganic nature is electricity - that disembodied energy that slumbers in the ultimate particles of matter - unseen, unfelt, unknown, till it suddenly leaps forth with such terrible vividness and power on the face of the storm, or till we summon it through the transformation of some other form of energy. A still higher and more inscrutable mystery is life - that something which clothes itself in such infinitely varied and beautiful as well as unbeautiful forms of matter. We can evoke electricity at will from many different sources, but we can evoke life only from other life; the biogenetic law is inviolable.

IV

It takes some of the cold iron out of the mechanistic theory of life if we divest it of all our associations with the machine-mad and machine-ridden world in which we live and out of which our material civilization came. The mechanical, the automatic, is the antithesis of the spontaneous and the poetic, and it repels us on that account. We are so made that the artificial systems please us far less than the natural systems. A sailing-ship takes us more than a steamship. It is nearer life, nearer the winged creatures. There is determinism in nature, mechanical forces are everywhere operative, but there are no machines in the proper sense of the word. When we call an organism a living machine we at once take it out of the categories of the merely mechanical and automatic and lift it into a higher order - the vital order.

Professor Le Dantec says we are mechanisms in the third degree, a mechanism of a mechanism of a mechanism. The body is a mechanism by virtue of its anatomy - its framework, its levers, its hinges; it is a mechanism by virtue of its chemical activities; and it is a mechanism by virtue of its colloid states - three kinds of mechanisms in one, and all acting together harmoniously and as a unit - in other words, a super-mechanical combination of activities.

The mechanical conception of life repels us because of its association in our minds with the fabrications of our own hands - the dead metal and wood and the noise and dust of our machine-ridden and machine-produced civilization.

But Nature makes no machines like our own. She uses mechanical principles everywhere, in inert matter and in living bodies, but she does not use them in the bald and literal way we do. We must divest her mechanisms of the rigidity and angularity that pertain to the works of our own hands. Her hooks and hinges and springs and sails and coils and aeroplanes, all involve mechanical contrivances, but how differently they impress us from our own application of the same principles! Even in inert matter - in the dews, the rains, the winds, the tides, the snows, the streams, - her mechanics and her chemistry and her hydrostatics and pneumatics, seem much nearer akin to life than our own. We must remember that Nature's machines are not human machines. When we place our machine so that it is driven by the great universal currents, - the wheel in the stream, the sail on the water, - the result is much more pleasing and poetic than when propelled by artificial power. The more machinery we get between ourselves and Nature, the farther off Nature seems. The marvels of crystallization, the beautiful vegetable forms which the frost etches upon the stone flagging of the sidewalk, and upon the window-pane, delight us and we do not reason why. A natural bridge pleases more than one which is the work of an engineer, yet the natural bridge can only stand when it is based upon good engineering principles. I found at the great Colorado Canon, that the more the monuments of erosion were suggestive of human structures, or engineering and architectural works, the more I was impressed by them. We are pleased when Nature imitates man, and we are pleased when man imitates Nature, and yet we recoil from the thought that life is only applied mechanics and chemistry. But the thought that it is mechanics and chemistry applied by something of which they as such, form no part, some agent or principle which we call vitality, is welcome to us. No machine we have ever made or seen can wind itself up, or has life, no chemical compound from the laboratories ever develops a bit of organic matter, and therefore we are disbelievers in the powers of these things.

V

Is gravity or chemical affinity any more real to the mind than vitality? Both are names for mysteries. Something which we call life lifts matter up, in opposition to gravity, into thousands of living forms. The tree lifts potash, silica, and lime up one or two hundred feet into the air; it elbows the soil away from its hole where it enters the ground; its roots split rocks. A giant sequoia lifts tons of solid matter and water up hundreds of feet. So will an explosion of powder or dynamite, but the tree does it slowly and silently by the organizing power of life. The vital is as inscrutably identified with the mechanical and chemical as the soul is identified with the body. They are one while yet they are two.

For purely mechanical things we can find equivalents. Arrest a purely mechanical process, and the machine only rests or rusts; arrest a vital process, and the machine evaporates, disintegrates, myriads of other machines reduce it to its original mineral and gaseous elements. In the organic world we strike a principle that is incalculable in its operation and incommensurable in its results. The physico-chemical forces we can bring to book; we know their orbits, their attractions and repulsions, and just what they will and will not do; we can forecast their movements and foresee their effects. But the vital forces transcend all our mathematics; we cannot anticipate their behavior. Start inert matter in motion and we know pretty nearly what will happen to it; mix the chemical elements together and we can foresee the results; but start processes or reactions we call life, and who can foresee the end? We know the sap will mount in the tree and the tree will be true to its type, but what do we or can we know of what it is that determines its kind and size? We know that in certain plants the leaves will always be opposite each other on the stalk, and that in other plants the leaves will alternate; that certain plants will have conspicuous and others inconspicuous flowers; but how can we know what it is in the cells of the plants that determines these things? We can graft the scion of a sour apple tree upon a sweet, and *vice versa*, and the fruit of the scion will be true to its kind, but no analysis of the scion or of the stock will reveal the secret, as it would in the case of chemical compounds. In inorganic nature we meet with concretions, but not secretions; with crystallization, but not with assimilation and growth from within. Chemistry tells us that the composition of animal bodies is identical with that of vegetable; that there is nothing in one that is not in the other; and yet, behold the difference! a difference beyond the reach of chemistry to explain. Biology can tell us all about these differences and many other things, but it cannot tell us the secret we are looking for, - what it is that fashions from the same elements two bodies so unlike as a tree and a man.

Decay and disintegration in the inorganic world often lead to the production of beautiful forms. In life the reverse is true; the vital forces build up varied and picturesque forms which when pulled down are shapeless and displeasing. The immense layers of sandstone and limestone out of which the wonderful forms that fill the Grand Canon of the Colorado are carved were laid down in wide uniform sheets; if the waters had deposited their material in the forms which we now see, it would have been a miracle. We marvel and admire as we gaze upon them now; we do more, we have to speculate as to how it was all done by the blind, unintelligent forces. Giant stairways, enormous alcoves, dizzy, highly wrought balustrades, massive vertical walls standing four-square like huge foundations - how did all the unguided erosive forces do it? The secret is in the structure of the rock, in the lines of cleavage, in the unequal hardness, and in the impulsive, irregular, and unequal action of the eroding agents. These agents follow the lines of least resistance; they are active at different times and seasons, and from different directions; they work with infinite slowness; they undermine, they disintegrate, they dislodge, they transport; the hard streaks resist them, the soft streaks invite them; water charged with sand and gravel saws down; the wind, armed with fine sand, rounds off and hollows out; and thus the sculpturing goes on. But after you have reasoned out all these things, you still marvel at the symmetry and the structural beauty of the forms. They look like the handiwork of barbarian gods. They are the handiwork of physical forces which we can see and measure and in a degree control. But what a gulf separates them from the handiwork of the organic forces!

VI

Some things come and some things arise; things that already exist may come, but potential things arise; my friend comes to visit me, the tide comes up the river, the cold or hot wave comes from the west; but the seasons, night and morning, health and disease, and the like, do not come in this sense; they arise. Life does not come to dead matter in this sense; it arises. Day and night are not traveling round the earth, though we view them that way; they arise from the turning of the earth upon its axis. If we could keep up with the flying moments, - that is, with the revolution of the earth, - we could live always at sunrise, or sunset, or at noon, or at any other moment we cared to elect. Love or hate does not come to our hearts; it is born there; the breath does not come to the newborn infant; respiration arises there automatically. See how the life of the infant is involved in that first breath, yet it is not its life; the infant must first be alive before it can breathe. If it is still-born, the respiratory reaction does not take place. We can say, then, that the breath means life, and the life means breath; only we must say the latter first. We can say in the same way that organization means life, and life means organization. Something sets up the organizing process in matter. We may take all the physical elements of life known to us and jumble them together and shake them up to all eternity, and life will not result. A little friction between solid bodies begets heat, a little more and we get fire. But no amount of friction begets life. Heat and life go together, but heat is the secondary factor.

Life is always a vanishing-point, a constant becoming - an unstable something that escapes us while we seem to analyze it. In its nature or essence, it is a metaphysical problem, and not one of physical science. Science cannot grasp it; it evaporates in its crucibles. And science is compelled finally to drive it into an imaginary region - I had almost said, metaphysical region, the region of the invisible, hypothetical atoms of matter. Here in the mysteries of molecular attraction and repulsion, it conceives the secret of life to lie.

John Burroughs

"Life is a wave," says Tyndall, but does not one conceive of something, some force or impulse in the wave that is not of the wave? What is it that travels along lifting new water each moment up into waves? It is a physical force communicated usually by the winds. When the wave dies upon the shore, this force is dissipated, not lost, or is turned into heat. Why may we not think of life as a vital force traveling through matter and lifting up into organic life waves in the same way? But not translatable into any other form of energy because not derivable from any other form.

Every species of animal has something about it that is unique and individual and that no chemical or physiological analysis of it will show - probably some mode of motion among its ultimate particles that is peculiar to itself. This prevents cross-breeding among different species and avoids a chaos of animal and vegetable forms. Living tissues and living organs from one species cannot be grafted upon the individuals of another species; the kidney of a cat, for instance, cannot be substituted for that of a dog, although the functions and the anatomy of the two are identical. It is suggested that an element of felineness and an element of canineness adhere in the cells of each, and the two are antagonistic. This specific quality, or selfness, of an animal pervades every drop of its blood, so that the blood relationship of the different forms may be thus tested, where chemistry is incompetent to show agreement or antagonism. The reactions of life are surer and more subtle than those of chemistry. Thus the blood relationship between birds and reptiles is clearly shown, as is the relationship of man and the chimpanzee and the orang-outang. The same general fact holds true in the vegetable world. You cannot graft the apple upon the oak, or the plum upon the elm. It seems as if there were the quality of oakness and the quality of appleness, and they would not mix.

The same thing holds among different chemical compounds. Substances which have precisely the same chemical formulae (called isomers) have properties as widely apart as alcohol and ether.

If chemistry is powerless to trace the relationship between different forms of life, is it not highly improbable that the secret of life itself is in the keeping of chemistry?

Analytical science has reached the end of its tether when it has resolved a body into its constituent elements. Why or how these elements build up a man in the one case, and a monkey in another, is beyond its province to say. It can deal with all the elements of the living body, vegetable and animal; it can take them apart and isolate them in different bottles; but it cannot put them together again as they were in life. It knows that the human body is built up of a vast multitude of minute cells, that these cells build tissues, that the tissues build organs, that the organs build the body; but the secret of the man, or the dog, or even the flea, is beyond its reach. The secret of biology, that which makes its laws and processes differ so widely from those of geology or astronomy, is a profound mystery. Science can take living tissue and make it grow outside of the body from which it came, but it will only repeat endlessly the first step of life - that of cell-multiplication; it is like a fire that will burn as long as fuel is given it and the ashes are removed; but it is entirely purposeless; it will not build up the organ of which it once formed a part, much less the whole organized body.

The difference between one man and another does not reside in his anatomy or physiology, or in the elements of which the brains and bodies are composed, but in something entirely beyond the reach of experimental science to disclose. The difference is psychological, or, we may say, philosophical, and science is none the wiser for it. The mechanics and the chemistry of a machine are quite sufficient to account for it, plus the man behind it. To the physics and chemistry of a living body, we are compelled to add some intangible, unknowable principle or tendency that physics and chemistry cannot disclose or define. One hesitates to make such a statement lest he do violence to that oneness, that sameness, that pervades the universe.

All trees go to the same soil for their ponderable elements, their ashes, and to the air and the light for their imponderable, - their carbon and their energy, - but what makes the tree, and makes one tree differ from another? Has the career of life upon this globe, the unfolding of the evolutionary process, been accounted for when you have named all the physical and material elements and processes which it involves? We take refuge in the phrase "the nature of things," but the nature of things evidently embraces something not dreamed of in our science.

It is reported that a French scientist has discovered the secret of the glow-worm's light. Of course it is a chemical reaction, - what else could it be? - but it is a chemical reaction in a vital process. Our mental and spiritual life - our emotions of art, poetry, religion - are inseparable from physical processes in the brain and the nervous system; but is that their final explanation? The sunlight has little effect on a withered leaf, but see what effect it has upon the green leaf upon the tree! The sunlight is the same, but it falls upon a new force or potency in the chlorophyll of the leaf, - a bit of chemistry there inspired by life, - and the heat of the sun is stored up in the carbon or woody tissues of the plant or tree, to be given out again in our stoves or fireplaces. And behold how much more of the solar heat is stored up in one kind of a tree than in certain other kinds, - how much in the hickory, oak, maple, and how little comparatively in the pine, spruce, linden, - all through the magic of something in the leaf, or shall we say of the spirit of the tree? If the laws of matter and force alone account for the living organism, if we do not have to think of something that organizes, then how do we account for the marvelous diversity of living forms, and their still more marvelous power of adaptation to changed conditions, since the laws of matter and force are the same everywhere? Science can deal only with the mechanism and chemistry of life, not with its essence; that which sets up the new activity in matter that we call vital is beyond its analysis. It is hard to believe that we have told the whole truth about a living body when we have enumerated all its chemical and mechanical activities. It is by such enumeration that we describe a watch, or a steam-engine, or any other piece of machinery. Describe I say, but such description does not account for the watch or tell us its full significance. To do this, we must include the watchmaker, and the world of mind and ideas amid which he lives. Now, in a living machine, the machine and the maker are one. The watch is perpetually self-wound and self-regulated and self-repaired. It is made up of millions of other little watches, the cells, all working together for one common end and ticking out the seconds and minutes of life with unfailing regularity. Unlike the watch we carry in our pockets, if we take it apart so as to stop its ticking, it can never be put together again. It has not merely stopped; it is dead.

The late William Keith Brooks, of Johns Hopkins University, said in opposition to Huxley that he held to the "old-fashioned conviction that living things do in some way, and in some degree, control or condition inorganic nature; that they hold their own by setting the mechanical properties of matter in opposition to each other, and that this is their most notable and distinctive characteristic." And yet, he said, to think of the living world as "anything but natural" is impossible.

VIII

Life seems to beget a new kind of chemistry, the same elements behave so differently when they are drawn into the life circuit from what they did before. Carbon, for instance, enters into hundreds of new compounds in the organic world that are unknown in the inorganic world. I am thus speaking of life as if it were something, some force or agent, that antedates its material manifestations, whereas in the eyes of science there is no separation of the one from the other. In an explosion there is usually something anterior to, or apart from, the explosive compound, that pulls the trigger, or touches the match, or completes the circuit, but in the slow and gentle explosions that keep the life machinery going, we cannot make such a distinction. The spark and the powder are one; the gun primes and fires itself; the battery is perpetually self-charged; the lamp is self-trimmed and self-lit.

Sir Oliver Lodge is apparently so impressed with some such considerations that he spiritualizes life, and makes it some mysterious entity in itself, existing apart from the matter which it animates and uses; not a source of energy but a timer and releaser of energy. Henri Bergson, in his "Creative Evolution," expounds a similar philosophy of life. Life is a current in opposition to matter which it enters into, and organizes into the myriads of living forms.

I confess that it is easier for me to think of life in these terms than in terms of physical science. The view falls in better with our anthropomorphic tendencies. It appeals to the imagination and to our myth-making aptitudes. It gives a dramatic interest to the question. With Bergson we see life struggling with matter, seeking to overcome its obduracy, compromising with it, taking a half-loaf when it cannot get a whole one; we see evolution as the unfolding of a vast drama acted upon the stage of geologic time. Creation becomes a perpetual process, the creative energy an ever-present and familiar fact. Bergson's book is a wonderful addition to the literature of science and of philosophy. The poet, the dreamer, the mystic, in each of us takes heart at Bergson's beautiful philosophy; it seems like a part of life; it goes so well with living things. As James said, it is like the light of the morning and the singing of birds; we glory in seeing the intellect humbled as he humbles it. The concepts of science try our mettle. They do not appeal to our humanity, or to our myth-making tendencies; they appeal to the purely intellectual, impersonal force within us. Though all our gods totter and fall, science goes its way; though our hearts are chilled and our lives are orphaned, science cannot turn aside, or veil its light. It does not temper the wind to the shorn lamb.

Hence the scientific conception of the universe repels many people. They are not equal to it. To think of life as involved in the very constitution of matter itself is a much harder proposition than to conceive of it as Bergson and Sir Oliver Lodge do, as an independent reality. The latter view gives the mind something more tangible to lay hold of. Indeed, science gives the mind nothing to take hold of. Does any chemical process give the mind any separate reality to take hold of? Is there a spirit of fire, or of decay, or of disease, or of health?

IX

Behold a man with his wonderful body, and still more wonderful mind; try to think of him as being fathered and mothered by the mere mechanical and chemical forces that we see at work in the rocks and soil underfoot, begotten by chemical affinity or the solar energy working as molecular physic, and mothered by the warmth and moisture, by osmosis and the colloid state - and all through the chance clashings and groupings of the irrational physical forces. Nothing is added to them, nothing guides or inspires them, nothing moves upon the face of the waters, nothing breathes upon the insensate clay. The molecules or corpuscles of the four principal elements - carbon, hydrogen, nitrogen, and oxygen - just happened to come together in certain definite numbers, and in a certain definite order, and invented or built up that most marvelous thing in the universe, the cell. The cells put their heads, or bodies, together, and built the tissues, the tissues formed the organs, the organs in convention assembled organized themselves into the body, and behold! A man, a bird, or a tree! - as chance a happening as the juxtaposition of the grains of sand upon the shore, or the shape of the summer clouds in the sky.

Aristotle dwells upon the internal necessity. The teeth of an animal arise from necessity, he says; the animal must have them in order to live. Yet it must have lived before it had them, else how would the necessity arise? If the horns of an animal arise from the same necessity, the changing conditions of its life begat the necessity; its life problem became more and more complicated, till new tools arose to meet new wants. But without some indwelling principle of development and progress, how could the new wants arise? Spencer says this progress is the result of the action and reaction between organisms and their changing environment. But you must first get your organism before the environment can work its effects, and you must have something in the organism that organizes and reacts from the environment. We see the agents he names astronomic, geologic, meteorologic, having their effects upon inanimate objects as well, but they do not start the process of development in them; they change a stone, but do not transform it into an organism. The chemist can take the living body apart as surely as the watchmaker can take a watch apart, but he cannot put the parts together again so that life will reappear, as the watchmaker can restore the time-keeping power of the watch. The watch is a mere mechanical contrivance with parts fitted to parts externally, while the living body is a mechanical and chemical contrivance, with parts blended with parts internally, so to speak, and acting together through sympathy, and not merely by mechanical adjustment. Do we not have to think of some organizing agent embracing and controlling all the parts, and integral in each of them, making a vital bond instead of a mechanical one?

There are degrees of vitality in living things, whereas there are only degrees of complexity and delicacy and efficiency in mechanical contrivances. One watch differs from another in the perfection of its works, but not as two living bodies with precisely similar structure differ from each other in their hold upon life, or in their measure of vitality. No analysis possible to science could show any difference in the chemistry and physics of two persons of whom one would withstand hardships and diseases that would kill the other, or with whom one would have the gift of long life and the other not. Machines differ from one another quantitatively - more or less efficiency; a living body differs from a machine qualitatively - its efficiency is of a different order; its unity is of a different order; its complexity is of a different order; the interdependence of its parts is of a different order. Yet what a parallel there is between a machine and a living body! Both are run by external forces or agents, solar energy in one applied mechanically from without; in the other applied vitally from within; both suffer from the wear and tear of time and from abuse, but one is self-repaired and the other powerless in this respect - two machines with the same treatment running the same number of years, but two men with the same treatment running a very unequal number of years. Machines of the same kind differ in durability, men differ in powers of endurance; a man can "screw up his courage," but a machine has no courage to screw up. Science may be unable to see any difference between vital mechanics, vital chemistry, and the chemics and mechanics of inorganic bodies - its analysis reveals no difference; but that there is a difference as between two different orders, all men see and feel.

Science cannot deal with fundamental questions. Only philosophy can do this. Science is only a tool or a key, and it can unlock only certain material problems. It cannot appraise itself. It is not a judge but a witness. Problems of mind, of character, moral, aesthetic, literary, artistic problems, are not its sphere. It counts and weighs and measures and analyzes, it traces relations, but it cannot appraise its own results. Science and religion come in conflict only when the latter seeks to deal with objective facts, and the former seeks to deal with subjective ideas and emotions. On the question of miracle they clash, because religion is then dealing with natural phenomena and challenges science. Philosophy offends science when it puts its own interpretation upon scientific facts. Science displeases literature when it dehumanizes nature and shows us irrefragable laws when we had looked for humanistic divinities.

John Burroughs

XI

THE ARRIVAL OF THE FIT

In my youth I once heard the then well-known lecturer Starr King speak on "The Law of Disorder." I have no recollection of the main thought of his discourse, but can see that it might have been upon the order and harmony that finally come out of the disharmonies of nature and of man. The whole universe goes blundering on, but surely arrives. Collisions and dispersions in the heavens above, and failure and destruction among living things on the earth below, yet here we all are in a world good to be in! The proof that it is good to be in is that we are actually here. It is as if the Creator played his right hand against his left - what one loses the other gains.

It has been aptly said that while Darwin's theory of natural selection may account for the survival of the fittest, it does not account for the arrival of the fittest. The arrival of the fittest, sooner or later, seems in some way guaranteed by tendencies that are beyond the hit-and-miss method of natural selection.

When we look back over the course of organic evolution, we see the unfolding of a great drama, or tragedy, in which, for millions upon millions of years the sole actors are low and all but brainless forms of life, devouring and devoured, in the old seas. We see, during other millions upon millions of years, a savage carnival of huge bestial forms upon the land, amphibian monsters and dragons of the land and air, devouring and being devoured, a riot of blood and carnage. We see the shifting of land and sea, the folding and crumpling of the earth's crust, the rise of mountains, the engulfing of forests, a vast destruction of life, immense numbers of animal forms becoming extinct through inability to adapt themselves to new conditions, or from other causes. We see creatures, half beast, half bird, or half dragon, half fish; we see the evolutionary process thwarted or delayed apparently by the hardening or fixing of its own forms. We see it groping its way like a blind man, and experimenting with this device and with that, fumbling, awkward, ineffectual, trying magnitude of body and physical strength first, and then shifting the emphasis to size of brain and delicacy and complexity of nerve-organization, pushing on but gropingly, learning only by experience, regardless of pain and waste and suffering; whole races of sentient beings swept away by some terrestrial cataclysm, as at the end of Palaeozoic and Mesozoic times; prodigal, inhuman, riotous, arming some vegetable growths with spurs and thorns that tear and stab, some insects with stings, some serpents with deadly fangs, the production of pain as much a part of the scheme of things as the production of pleasure; the creative impulse feeling its way through the mollusk to the fish, and through the fish to the amphibian and the reptile, through the reptile to the mammal, and through the mammal to the anthropoid apes, and through the apes to man, then through the rude and savage races of man, the long-jawed, small-brained, Pliocene man, hairy and savage, to the cave-dwellers and stone-implement man of Pleistocene times, and so on to our rude ancestors whom we see dimly at the dawn of history, and thus rapidly upward to the European man of our own era. What a record! What savagery, what thwartings and delays, what carnage and suffering, what an absence of all that we mean by intelligent planning and oversight, of love, of fatherhood! Just a clash of forces, the battle to the strong and the race to the fleet.

It is hard to believe that the course of organic evolution would have eventuated in man and the other higher forms of life without some guiding principle; yet it is equally difficult to believe that the course of any guiding intelligence down the

John Burroughs

ages would have been strewn with so many failures and monstrosities, so much waste and suffering and delay. Man has not been specially favored by one force or element in nature. Behold the enemies that beset him without and within, and that are armed for his destruction! The intelligence that appears to pervade the organic world, and that reaches its conscious expression in the brain of man, is just as manifest in all the forms of animals and plants that are inimical to him, in all his natural enemies, - venomous snakes and beasts of prey, and insect pests, - as in anything else. Nature is as wise and solicitous for rats and mice as for men. In fact, she has endowed many of the lower creatures with physical powers that she has denied him. Evidently man is only one of the cards in her pack; doubtless the highest one, but the game is not played for him alone.

There is no economy of effort or of material in nature as a whole, whatever there may be in special parts. The universe is not run on modern business-efficiency principles. There is no question of time, or of profit, of solvency or insolvency. The profit-and-loss account in the long run always balances. In our astronomic age there are probably vastly more dead suns and planets strewing the depths of sidereal space than there are living suns and planets. But in some earlier period in the cycle of time the reverse may have been true, or it may be true in some future period.

There is economy of effort in the individual organism, but not in the organic series, at least from the human point of view. During the biologic ages there have been a vast number of animal forms, great and small, and are still, that had no relation to man, that were not in his line of descent, and played no part in his evolution. During that carnival of monstrous and gigantic forms in Mesozoic time the ancestor of man was probably some small and insignificant creature whose life was constantly imperiled by the huge beasts about it. That it survived at all in the clash of forces, bestial and elemental, during those early ages, is one of the wonders of time. The drama or tragedy of evolution has had many actors, some of them fearful and terrible to look upon, who have played their parts and passed off the stage, as if the sole purpose was the entertainment of some unseen spectator. When we reach human history, what wasted effort, what failures, what blind groping, what futile undertakings! - war, famine, pestilence, delaying progress or bringing to naught the wisdom of generations of men! Those who live in this age are witnessing in the terrible European war something analogous to the blind, wasteful fury of the elemental forces; millions of men who never saw one another, and who have not the shadow of a quarrel, engage in a life-and-death struggle, armed with all the aids that centuries of science and civilization can give them - a tragedy that darkens the very heavens and makes a mockery of all our age-old gospel of peace and good will to men. It is a catastrophe on a scale with the cataclysms of geologic time when whole races disappeared and the face of continents was changed. It seems that men in the aggregate, with all their science and religion, are no more exempt from the operation of cosmic laws than are the stocks and stones. Each party to this gigantic struggle declares that he is in it against his will; the fate that rules in the solar system seems to have them all in its grip; the working of forces and tendencies for which no man was responsible seems to have brought it about. Social communities grow in grace and good-fellowship, but governments in their relations to one another, and often in relation to their own subjects, are still barbarous. Men become christianized, but man is still a heathen, the victim of savage instincts. In this struggle one of the most admirable and efficient of nations, and one of the most solicitous for the lives and well-being of its citizens, is suddenly seized with a fury of destruction, hurling its soldiers to death as if they were only the waste of the fields, and trampling down other peoples whose geographic position placed them in their way as if they were merely vermin, throwing international morality to the winds, looking upon treaties as "scraps of paper," regarding themselves as the salt of the earth, the chosen of the Lord, appropriating the Supreme Being as did the colossal egotism of old Israel, and quickly getting down to the basic principle of savage life - that might makes right.

Little wonder that the good people are asking, Have we lost faith? We may or we may not have lost faith, but can we not see that our faith does not give us a key to the problem? Our faith is founded on the old prescientific conception of a universe in which good and evil are struggling with each other, with a Supreme Being aiding and abetting the good. We fail to appreciate that the cosmic laws are no respecters of persons. Emerson says there is no god dare wrong a worm, but worms dare wrong one another, and there is no god dare take sides with either. The tides in the affairs of men are as little subject to human control as the tides of the sea and the air. We may fix the blame of the European war upon this government or upon that, but race antagonisms and geographical position are not matters of choice. An island empire, like England, is bound to be jealous of all rivals upon the sea, because her very life, when nations clash, depends upon her control of it; and an inland empire, like Germany, is bound to grow restless under the pressure of contiguous states of other races. A vast empire, like Russia, is always in danger of falling apart by its own weight. It is fused and consolidated by a turn of events that arouse the patriotic emotions of the whole people and unite them in a common enthusiasm.

The evolution of nations is attended by the same contingencies, the same law of probability, the same law of the survival of the fit, as are organic bodies. I say the survival of the fit; there are degrees of fitness in the scale of life; the fit survive, and the fittest lead and dominate, as did the reptiles in Mesozoic time, and the mammals in Tertiary time. Among the mammals man is dominant because he is the fittest. Nations break up or become extinct when they are no longer fit, or equal to the exigencies of the struggles of life. The Roman Empire would still exist if it had been entirely fit. The causes of its unfitness form a long and intricate problem. Germany of to-day evidently looks upon herself as the dominant nation, the one fittest to survive, and she has committed herself to the desperate struggle of justifying her self-estimate. She tramples down weaker nations as we do the stubble of the fields. She would plough and harrow the world to plant her Prussian

Kultur. This *Kultur* is a mighty good product, but we outside of its pale think that French *Kultur*, and English *Kultur*, and American *Kultur* are good products also, and equally fit to survive. We naturally object to being ploughed under. That Russian *Kultur* has so far proved itself a vastly inferior product cannot be doubted, but the evolutionary processes will in time bring a finer and higher Russia out of this vast weltering and fermenting mass of humanity. In all these things impersonal laws and forces are at work, and the balance of power, if temporarily disturbed, is bound, sooner or later, to be restored just as it is in the inorganic realm.

Evolution is creative, as Bergson contends. The wonder is that, notwithstanding the indifference of the elemental forces and the blind clashing of opposing tendencies among living forms, - a universe that seems run entirely on the trial-and-error principle, - evolution has gone steadily forward, a certain order and stability has been reached in the world of inert bodies and forces, and myriads of forms of wonderful fitness and beauty have been reached in the organic realm. Just as the water-system and the weather-system of the globe have worked them-selves out on the hit-and-miss plan, but not without serious defects, - much too much water and heat at a few places, and much too little at a few others, - so the organic impulse, warred upon by the blind inorganic elements and preyed upon by the forms it gave rise to, has worked itself out and peopled the world as we see it peopled to-day - not with forms altogether admirable and lovely from our point of view, but so from the point of view of the whole. The forests get themselves planted by the go-as-you-please winds and currents, the pines in one place, the spruce, the oaks, the elms, the beeches, in another, all with a certain fitness and system. The waters gather themselves together in great bodies and breathe salubrity and fertility upon the land.

A certain order and reasonableness emerges from the chaos and cross-purposes. There are harmony and cooeperation among the elemental forces, as well as strife and antagonism. Life gets on, for all groping and blundering. There is the inherent variability of living forms to begin with - the primordial push toward the development from within which, so far as we can see, is not fortuitous, but predestined; and there is the stream of influences from without, constantly playing upon and modifying the organism and taken advantage of by it.

The essence of life is in adaptability; it goes into partnership with the forces and conditions that surround it. It is this trait which leads the teleological philosopher to celebrate the fitness of the environment when its fitness is a foregone conclusion. Shall we praise the fitness of the air for breathing, or of the water for drinking, or of the winds for filling our sails? If we cannot say explicitly, without speaking from our anthropomorphism, that there is a guiding intelligence in the evolution of living forms, we can at least say, I think, that the struggle for life is favored by the very constitution of the universe and that man in some inscrutable way was potential in the fiery nebula itself.

XII

THE NATURALIST'S VIEW OF LIFE

I

William James said that one of the privileges of a philosopher was to contradict other philosophers. I may add in the same spirit that one of the fatalities of many philosophers is, sooner or later, to contradict themselves. I do not know that James ever contradicted himself, but I have little doubt that a critical examination of his works would show that he sometimes did so; I remember that he said he often had trouble to make both ends of his philosophy meet. Any man who seeks to compass any of the fundamental problems with the little span of his finite mind, is bound at times to have trouble to make both ends meet. The man of science seldom has any such trouble with his problems; he usually knows what is the matter and forthwith seeks to remedy it. But the philosopher works with a much more intangible and elusive material, and is lucky if he is ever aware when both ends fail to meet.

I have often wondered if Darwin, who was a great philosopher as well as a great man of science, saw or felt the contradiction between his theory of the origin of species through natural selection working upon fortuitous variations, and his statement, made in his old age, that he could not look upon man, with all his wonderful powers, as the result of mere chance. The result of chance man certainly is - is he not? - as are all other forms of life, if evolution is a mere mechanical process set going and kept going by the hit-and-miss action of the environment upon the organism, or by the struggle for existence. If evolution involves no intelligence in nature, no guiding or animating principle, then is not man an accidental outcome of the blind clashing and jolting of the material forces, as much so as the great stone face in the rocks which Hawthorne used so suggestively in one of his stories?

I have wondered if Huxley was aware that both ends of his argument did not quite meet when he contended for the truth of determinism - that there is and can be no free or spontaneous volition; and at the same time set man apart from the cosmic order, and represented him as working his will upon it, crossing and reversing its processes. In one of his earlier essays, Huxley said that to the student of living things, as contrasted with the student of inert matter, the aspect of nature is reversed. "In living matter, incessant, and so far as we know, spontaneous, change is the rule, rest the exception, the anomaly, to be accounted for. Living things have no inertia, and tend to no equilibrium," except the equilibrium of death. This is good vitalistic doctrine, as far as it goes, yet Huxley saw no difference between the matter of life and other matter, except in the manner in which the atoms are aggregated. Probably the only difference between a diamond and a piece of charcoal, or between a pearl and an oyster-shell, is the manner in which the atoms are aggregated; but that the secret of life is in the peculiar compounding of the atoms or molecules - a spatial arrangement of them - is a harder proposition. It seems to me also that Haeckel involves himself in obvious contra- dictions when he ascribes will, sensation, inclination, dislike, though of a low order, to the atoms of matter; in fact, sees them as living beings with souls, and then denies soul, will, power of choice, and the like to their collective unity in the brain of man.

A philosopher cannot well afford to assume the air of lofty indifference that the poet Whitman does when he asks, "Do I contradict myself? Very well, then, I contradict myself"; but he may take comfort in the thought that contradictions are often only apparent, and not real, as when two men standing on opposite sides of the earth seem to oppose each other, and yet their heads point to the same heavens, and their feet to the same terrestrial centre. The logic of the earth completely contradicts the ideas we draw from our experience with other globes, both our artificial globes and the globes in the forms of the sun and the moon that we see in the heavens. The earth has only one side, the outside, which is always the upper side; at the South Pole, as at the North, we are on the top side. I fancy the whole truth of any of the great problems, if we could see it, would reconcile all our half-truths, all the contradictions in our philosophy.

In considering this problem of the mystery of living things, I have had a good deal of trouble in trying to make my inborn idealism go hand in hand with my inborn naturalism; but I am not certain that there is any real break or contradiction between them, only a surface one, and that deeper down the strata still unite them. Life seems beyond the capacity of inorganic nature to produce; and yet here is life in its myriad forms, here is the body and mind of man, and here is the world of inanimate matter out of which all living beings arise, and into which they sooner or later return; and we must either introduce a new principle to account for it all, or else hold to the idea that what is is natural - a legitimate outcome of the universal laws and processes that have been operating through all time. This last is the point of view of the present chapter, - the point of view of naturalism; not strictly the scientific view which aims to explain all life phenomena in terms of exact experimental science, but the larger, freer view of the open-air naturalist and literary philosopher. I cannot get rid of, or hold in abeyance, my inevitable idealism, if I would; neither can I do violence to my equally inevitable naturalism, but may I not hope to make the face of my naturalism beam with the light of the ideal - the light that never was in the physico-chemical order, and never can be there?

II

The naturalist cannot get away from the natural order, and he sees man, and all other forms of life, as an integral part of it - the order, which in inert matter is automatic and fateful, and which in living matter is prophetic and indeterminate; the course of one down the geologic ages, seeking only a mechanical repose, being marked by collisions and disruptions; the other in its course down the biologic ages seeking a vital and unstable repose, being marked by pain, failure, carnage, extinction, and ceaseless struggle with the physical order upon which it depends. Man has taken his chances in the clash of blind matter, and in the warfare of living forms. He has been the pet of no god, the favorite of no power on earth or in heaven. He is one of the fruits of the great cosmic tree, and is subject to the same hazards and failures as the fruit of all other trees. The frosts may nip him in the bud, the storms beat him down, foes of earth and air prey upon him, and hostile influences from all sides impede or mar him. The very forces that uphold him and furnish him his armory of tools and of power, will destroy him the moment he is off his guard. He is like the trainer of wild beasts who, at his peril, for one instant relaxes his mastery over them. Gravity, electricity, fire, flood, hurricane, will crush or consume him if his hand is unsteady or his wits tardy. Nature has dealt with him upon the same terms as with all other forms of life. She has shown him no favor. The same elements - the same water, air, lime, iron, sulphur, oxygen, carbon, and so on - make up his body and his brain as make up theirs, and the same make up theirs as are the constituents of the insensate rocks, soils, and clouds. The same elements, the same atoms and molecules, but a different order; the same solar energy, but working to other ends; the same life principle but lifted to a higher plane. How can we separate man from the total system of things, setting him upon one side and them upon another, making the relation of the two mechanical or accidental? It is only in thought, or in obedience to some creed or philosophy, that we do it. In life, in action, we unconsciously recognize ourselves as a part of Nature. Our

success and well-being depend upon the closeness and sponta-
neousness of the relation.

If all this is interpreted to mean that life, that the mind and
soul of man, are of material origin, science does not shrink
from the inference. Only the inference demands a newer and
higher conception of matter - the conception that Tyndall
expressed when he wrote the word with a capital M, and
declared that Matter was "at bottom essentially mystical and
transcendental"; that Goethe expressed when he called matter
"the living garment of God"; and that Whitman expressed
when he said that the soul and the body were one. The
materialism of the great seers and prophets of science who
penetrate into the true inwardness of matter, who see through
the veil of its gross obstructive forms and behold it translated
into pure energy, need disturb no one.

In our religious culture we have beggared matter that we might
exalt spirit; we have bankrupted earth that we might enrich
heaven; we have debased the body that we might glorify the
soul. But science has changed all this. Mankind can never
again rest in the old crude dualism. The Devil has had his day,
and the terrible Hebrew Jehovah has had his day; the divinities
of this world are now having their day.

The puzzle or the contradiction in the naturalistic view of life
appears when we try to think of a being as a part of Nature,
having his genesis in her material forces, who is yet able to
master and direct Nature, reversing her processes and defeating
her ends, opposing his will to her fatalism, his mercy to her
cruelty - in short, a being who thinks, dreams, aspires, loves
truth, justice, goodness, and sits in judgment upon the very
gods he worships. Must he not bring a new force, an alien
power? Can a part be greater than the whole? Can the psychic
dominate the physical out of which it came? Again we have
only to enlarge our conception of the physical - the natural - or
make our faith measure up to the demands of reason. Our
reason demands that the natural order be all-inclusive. Can our
faith in the divinity of matter measure up to this standard? Not

till we free ourselves from the inherited prejudices which have grown up from our everyday struggles with gross matter. We must follow the guidance of science till we penetrate this husk and see its real mystical and transcendental character, as Tyndall did.

When we have followed matter from mass to molecule, from molecule to atom, from atom to electron, and seen it in effect dematerialized, - seen it in its fourth or ethereal, I had almost said spiritual, state, - when we have grasped the wonder of radio-activity, and the atomic transformations that attend it, we shall have a conception of the potencies and possibilities of matter that robs scientific materialism of most of its ugliness. Of course, no deductions of science can satisfy our longings for something kindred to our own spirits in the universe. But neither our telescopes nor our microscopes reveal such a reality. Is this longing only the result of our inevitable anthropomorphism, or is it the evidence of things unseen, the substance of things hoped for, the prophecy of our kinship with the farthest star? Can soul arise out of a soulless universe?

Though the secret of life is under our feet, yet how strange and mysterious it seems! It draws our attention away from matter. It arises among the inorganic elements like a visitant from another sphere. It is a new thing in the world. Consciousness is a new thing, yet Huxley makes it one of his trinity of realities - matter, energy, and consciousness. We are so immersed in these realities that we do not see the divinity they embody. We call that sacred and divine which is far off and unattainable. Life and mind are so impossible of explanation in terms of matter and energy, that it is not to be wondered at that mankind has so long looked upon their appearance upon this earth as a miraculous event. But until science opened our eyes we did not know that the celestial and the terrestrial are one, and that we are already in the heavens among the stars. When we emancipate ourselves from the bondage of wont and use, and see with clear vision our relations to the Cosmos, all our ideas of materialism and spiritualism are made over, and we see how the two are one; how life and death play into each other's hands, and how the whole truth of things cannot be compassed by any number of finite minds.

John Burroughs

III

When we are bold enough to ask the question, Is life an addition to matter or an evolution from matter? how all these extra-scientific theories about life as a separate entity wilt and fade away! If we know anything about the ways of creative energy, we know that they are not as our ways; we know its processes bear no analogy to the linear and external doings of man. Creative energy works from within; it identifies itself with, and is inseparable from, the element in which it works. I know that in this very statement I am idealizing the creative energy, but my reader will, I trust, excuse this inevitable anthropomorphism. The way of the creative energy is the way of evolution. When we begin to introduce things, when we begin to separate the two orders, the vital and the material, or, as Bergson says, when we begin to think of things created, and of a thing that creates, we are not far from the state of mind of our childhood, and of the childhood of the race. We are not far from the Mosaic account of creation. Life appears as an introduction, man and his soul as introductions.

Our reason, our knowledge of the method of Nature, declare for evolution; because here we are, here is this amazing world of life about us, and here it goes on through the action and interaction of purely physical and chemical forces. Life seems as natural as day and night, as the dews and the rain. Our studies of the past history of the globe reveal the fact that life appeared upon a cooling planet when the temperature was suitable, and when its basic elements, water and carbon dioxide, were at hand. How it began, whether through insensible changes in the activities of inert matter, lasting whole geologic ages, or by a sudden transformation at many points on the earth's surface, we can never know. But science can see no reason for believing that its beginning was other than natural; it was inevitable from the constitution of matter itself. Moreover, since the law of evolution seems of universal application, and affords the key to more great problems than any other generalization of the human mind, one would say on *a priori* grounds that life is an evolution, that its genesis is to be sought in the inherent capacities and potentialities of matter itself. How else could it come? Science cannot go outside of matter and its laws for an explanation of any phenomena that appear in matter. It goes inside of matter instead, and in its mysterious molecular attractions and repulsions, in the whirl and dance of the atoms and electrons, in their emanations and transformations, in their amazing potencies and activities, sees, or seems to see, the secret of the origin of life itself. But this view is distasteful to a large number of thinking persons. Many would call it frank materialism, and declare that it is utterly inadequate to supply the spiritual and ideal background which is the strength and solace of our human life.

John Burroughs

IV

The lay mind can hardly appreciate the necessity under which the man of science feels to account for all the phenomena of life in terms of the natural order. To the scientist the universe is complete in itself. He can admit of no break or discontinuity anywhere. Threads of relation, visible and invisible, - chemical, mechanical, electric, magnetic, solar, lunar, stellar, geologic, biologic, - forming an intricate web of subtle forces and influences, bind all things, living and dead, into a cosmic unity. Creation is one, and that one is symbolized by the sphere which rests forever on itself, which is whole at every point, which holds all forms, which reconciles all contradictions, which has no beginning and no ending, which has no upper and no under, and all of whose lines are fluid and continuous. The disruptions and antagonisms which we fancy we see are only the result of our limited vision; nature is not at war with itself; there is no room or need for miracle; there is no outside to the universe, because there are no bounds to matter or spirit; all is inside; deep beneath deep, height above height, and this mystery and miracle that we call life must arise out of the natural order in the course of time as inevitably as the dew forms and the rain falls. When the rains and the dews and the snows cease to fall, - a time which science predicts, - then life, as we know it, must inevitably vanish from the earth. Human life is a physical phenomenon, and though it involves, as we believe, a psychic or non-physical principle, it is still not exempt from the operation of the universal physical laws. It came by them or through them, and it must go by them or through them.

The rigidly scientific mind, impressed with all these things as the lay mind cannot be, used to the searching laboratory methods, and familiar with the phenomenon of life in its very roots, as it were, dealing with the wonders of chemical compounds, and the forces that lurk in molecules and atoms, seeing in the cosmic universe, and in the evolution of the earth, only the operation of mechanical and chemical principles; seeing the irrefragable law of the correlation and the conservation of forces; tracing consciousness and all our changes in mental states to changes in the brain substance; drilled in methods of proof by experimentation; knowing that the same number of ultimate atoms may be so combined or married as to produce compounds that differ as radically as alcohol and ether, - conversant with all these things, and more, I say, - the strictly scientific mind falls naturally and inevitably into the mechanistic conception of all life phenomena.

Science traces the chain of cause and effect everywhere and finds no break. It follows down animal life till it merges in the vegetable, though it cannot put its finger or its microscope on the point where one ends and the other begins. It finds forms that partake of the characteristics of both. It is reasonable to expect that the vegetable merges into the mineral by the same insensible degrees, and that the one becomes the other without any real discontinuity. The change, if we may call it such, probably takes place in the interior world of matter among the primordial atoms, where only the imagination can penetrate. In that sleep of the ultimate corpuscle, what dreams may come, what miracles may be wrought, what transformations take place! When I try to think of life as a mode of motion in matter, I seem to see the particles in a mystic dance, a whirling maze of motions, the infinitely little people taking hold of hands, changing partners, facing this way and that, doing all sorts of impossible things, like jumping down one another's throats, or occupying one another's bodies, thrilled and vibrating at an inconceivable rate.

The theological solution of this problem of life fails more and more to satisfy thinking men of to-day. Living things are natural phenomena, and we feel that they must in some way be an outcome of the natural order. Science is more and more familiarizing our minds with the idea that the universe is a universe, a oneness; that its laws are continuous. We follow the chemistry of it to the farthest stars and there is no serious break or exception; it is all of one stuff. We follow the mechanics of it into the same abysmal depths, and there are no breaks or exceptions. The biology of it we cannot follow beyond our own little corner of the universe; indeed, we have no proof that there is any biology anywhere else. But if there is, it must be similar to our own. There is only one kind of electricity (though two phases of it), only one kind of light and heat, one kind of chemical affinity, in the universe; and hence only one kind of life. Looked at in its relation to the whole, life appears like a transient phenomenon of matter. I will not say accidental; it seems inseparably bound up with the cosmic processes, but, I may say, fugitive, superficial, circumscribed. Life comes and goes; it penetrates but a little way into the earth; it is confined to a certain range of temperature. Beyond a certain degree of cold, on the one hand, it does not appear; and beyond a certain degree of heat, on the other, it is cut off. Without water or moisture, it ceases; and without air, it is not. It has evidently disappeared from the moon, and probably from the inferior planets, and it is doubtful if it has yet appeared on any of the superior planets, save Mars.

Life comes to matter as the flowers come in the spring, - when the time is ripe for it, - and it disappears when the time is over-ripe. Man appears in due course and has his little day upon the earth, but that day must as surely come to an end. Yet can we conceive of the end of the physical order? the end of gravity? or of cohesion? The air may disappear, the water may disappear, combustion may cease; but oxygen, hydrogen, nitrogen, and carbon will continue somewhere.

V

Science is the redeemer of the physical world. It opens our eyes to its true inwardness, and purges it of the coarse and brutal qualities with which, in our practical lives, it is associated. It has its inner world of activities and possibilities of which our senses give us no hint. This inner world of molecules and atoms and electrons, thrilled and vibrating with energy, the infinitely little, the almost infinitely rapid, in the bosom of the infinitely vast and distant and automatic - what a revelation it all is! what a glimpse into "Nature's infinite book of secrecy"!

Our senses reveal to us but one kind of motion - mass motion - the change of place of visible bodies. But there is another motion in all matter which our senses do not reveal to us as motion - molecular vibration, or the thrill of the atoms. At the heart of the most massive rock this whirl of the atoms or corpuscles is going on. If our ears were fine enough to hear it, probably every rock and granite monument would sing, as did Memnon, when the sun shone upon it. This molecular vibration is revealed to us as heat, light, sound, electricity. Heat is only a mode of this invisible motion of the particles of matter. Mass motion is quickly converted into this molecular motion when two bodies strike each other. May not life itself be the outcome of a peculiar whirl of the ultimate atoms of matter?

Says Professor Gotch, as quoted by J. Arthur Thomson in his "Introduction to Science": "To the thought of a scientific mind the universe with all its suns and worlds is throughout one seething welter of modes of motion, playing in space, playing in ether, playing in all existing matter, playing in all living things, playing, therefore, in ourselves." Physical science, as Professor Thomson says, leads us from our static way of looking at things to the dynamic way. It teaches us to regard the atom, not as a fixed and motionless structure, like the bricks in a wall, but as a centre of ever-moving energy; it sees the whole universe is in a state of perpetual flux, a flowing stream of creative energy out of which life arises as one of the manifestations of this energy.

When we have learned all that science can tell us about the earth, is it not more rather than less wonderful? When we know all it can tell us about the heavens above, or about the sea, or about our own bodies, or about a flower, or a bird, or a tree, or a cloud, are they less beautiful and wonderful? The mysteries of generation, of inheritance, of cell life, are rather enhanced by science.

VI

When the man of science seeks to understand and explain the world in which we live, he guards himself against seeing double, or seeing two worlds instead of one, as our unscientific fathers did - an immaterial or spiritual world surrounding and interpenetrating the physical world, or the supernatural enveloping and directing the natural. He sees but one world, and that a world complete in itself; surrounded, it is true, by invisible forces, and holding immeasured and immeasurable potencies; a vastly more complex and wonderful world than our fathers ever dreamed of; a fruit, as it were, of the great sidereal tree, bound by natal bonds to myriads of other worlds, of one stuff with them, ahead or behind them in its ripening, but still complete in itself, needing no miracle to explain it, no spirits or demons to account for its processes, not even its vital processes.

In the light of what he knows of the past history of the earth, the man of science sees with his mind's eye the successive changes that have taken place in it; he sees the globe a mass of incandescent matter rolling through space; he sees the crust cooling and hardening; he sees the waters appear, the air and the soil appear, he sees the clouds begin to form and the rain to fall, he sees living things appear in the waters, then upon the land, and in the air; he sees the two forms of life arise, the vegetable and the animal, the latter standing upon the former; he sees more and more complex forms of both vegetable and animal arise and cover the earth. They all appear in the course of the geologic ages on the surface of the earth; they arise out of it; they are a part of it; they come naturally; no hand reaches down from heaven and places them there; they are not an addendum; they are not a sudden creation; they are an evolution; they were potential in the earth before they arose out of it. The earth ripened, her crust mellowed, and thickened, her airs softened and cleared, her waters were purified, and in due time her finer fruits were evolved, and, last of all, man arose. It was all one process. There was no miracle, no first day of creation; all were days of creation. Brooded by the sun, the earth hatched her offspring; the promise and the potency of all terrestrial life was in the earth herself; her womb was fertile from the first. All that we call the spiritual, the divine, the celestial, were hers, because man is hers. Our religions and our philosophies and our literatures are hers; man is a part of the whole system of things; he is not an alien, nor an accident, nor an interloper; he is here as the rains, the dews, the flowers, the rocks, the soil, the trees, are here. He appeared when the time was ripe, and he will disappear when the time is over-ripe. He is of the same stuff as the ground he walks upon; there is no better stuff in the heavens above him, nor in the depths below him, than sticks to his own ribs. The celestial and the terrestrial forces unite and work together in him, as in all other creatures. We cannot magnify man without magnifying the universe of which he is a part; and we cannot belittle it without belittling him.

Now we can turn all this about and look upon it as mankind looked upon it in the prescientific ages, and as so many persons still look upon it, and think of it all as the work of external and higher powers. We can think of the earth as the footstool of some god, or the sport of some demon; we can people the earth and the air with innumerable spirits, high and low; we can think of life as something apart from matter. But science will not, cannot follow us; it cannot discredit the world it has disclosed - I had almost said, the world it has created. Science has made us at home in the universe. It has visited the farthest stars with its telescope and spectroscope, and finds we are all akin. It has sounded the depths of matter with its analysis, and it finds nothing alien to our own bodies. It sees motion everywhere, motion within motion, transformation, metamorphosis everywhere, energy everywhere, currents and counter-currents everywhere, ceaseless change everywhere; it finds nothing in the heavens more spiritual, more mysterious, more celestial, more godlike, than it finds upon this earth. This does not imply that evolution may not have progressed farther upon other worlds, and given rise to a higher order of intelligences than here; it only implies that creation is one, and that the same forces, the same elements and possibilities, exist everywhere.

VII

Give free rein to our anthropomorphic tendencies, and we fill the world with spirits, good and bad - bad in war, famine, pestilence, disease; good in all the events and fortunes that favor us. Early man did this on all occasions; he read his own hopes and fears and passions into all the operations of nature. Our fathers did it in many things; good people of our own time do it in exceptional instances, and credit any good fortune to Providence. Men high in the intellectual and philosophical world, still invoke something antithetical to matter, to account for the appearance of life on the planet.

It may be justly urged that the effect upon our habits of thought of the long ages during which this process has been going on, leading us to differentiate matter and spirit and look upon them as two opposite entities, hindering or contending with each other, - one heavenly, the other earthly, one everlasting, the other perishable, one the supreme good, the other the seat and parent of all that is evil, - the cumulative effect of this habit of thought in the race-mind is, I say, not easily changed or overcome. We still think, and probably many of us always will think, of spirit as something alien to matter, something mystical, transcendental, and not of this world. We look upon matter as gross, obstructive, and the enemy of the spirit. We do not know how we are going to get along without it, but we solace ourselves with the thought that by and by, in some other, non-material world, we shall get along without it, and experience a great expansion of life by reason of our emancipation from it. Our practical life upon this planet is more or less a struggle with gross matter; our senses apprehend it coarsely; of its true inwardness they tell us nothing; of the perpetual change and transformation of energy going on in bodies about us they tell us nothing; of the wonders and potencies of matter as revealed in radio-activity, in the X-ray, in chemical affinity and polarity, they tell us nothing; of the all-pervasive ether, without which we could not see or live at all, they tell us nothing. In fact we live and move and have our being in a complex of forces and tendencies of which, even by the aid of science, we but see as through a glass darkly. Of the effluence of things, the emanations from the minds and bodies of our friends, and from other living forms about us, from the heavens above and from the earth below, our daily lives tell us nothing, any more than our eyes tell us of the invisible rays in the sun's spectrum, or than our ears tell us of the murmurs of the life-currents in growing things. Science alone unveils the hidden wonders and sleepless activities of the world forces that play through us and about us. It alone brings the heavens near, and reveals the brotherhood or sisterhood of worlds. It alone makes man at home in the universe, and shows us how many friendly powers wait upon him day and night. It alone shows him the glories and the wonders of the voyage we are making upon this ship in the stellar infinitude, and that, whatever the port, we shall still be on familiar ground - we cannot get away from home.

There is always an activity in inert matter that we little suspect. See the processes going on in the stratified rocks that suggest or parody those of life. See the particles of silica that are diffused through the limestone, hunting out each other and coming together in concretions and forming flint or chert nodules; or see them in the process of petrifaction slowly building up a tree of chalcedony or onyx in place of a tree of wood, repeating every cell, every knot, every worm-hole - dead matter copying exactly a form of living matter; or see the phenomenon of crystallization everywhere; see the solution of salt mimicking, as Tyndall says, the architecture of Egypt, building up miniature pyramids, terrace upon terrace, from base to apex, forming a series of steps like those up which the traveler in Egypt is dragged by his guides! We can fancy, if we like, these infinitesimal structures built by an invisible population which swarms among the constituent molecules, controlled and coerced by some invisible matter, says Tyndall. This might be called literature, or poetry, or religion, but it would not be science; science says that these salt pyramids are the result of the play of attraction and repulsion among the salt molecules themselves; that they are self-poised and self-quarried; it goes further than that and says that the quality we call saltness is the result of a certain definite arrangement of their ultimate atoms of matter; that the qualities of things as they affect our senses - hardness, softness, sweetness, bitterness - are the result of molecular motion and combination among the ultimate atoms. All these things seem on the threshold of life, waiting in the antechamber, as it were; to-morrow they will be life, or, as Tyndall says, "Incipient life, as it were, manifests itself throughout the whole of what is called inorganic nature."

VIII

The question of the nature and origin of life is a kind of perpetual motion question in biology. Life without antecedent life, so far as human experience goes, is an impossibility, and motion without previous motion, is equally impossible. Yet, while science shows us that this last is true among ponderable bodies where friction occurs, it is not true among the finer particles of matter, where friction does not exist. Here perpetual or spontaneous motion is the rule. The motions of the molecules of gases and liquids, and their vibrations in solids, are beyond the reach of our unaided senses, yet they are unceasing. By analogy we may infer that while living bodies, as we know them, do not and cannot originate spontaneously, yet the movement that we call life may and probably does take place spontaneously in the ultimate particles of matter. But can atomic energy be translated into the motion of ponderable bodies, or mass energy? In like manner can, or does, this potential life of the world of atoms and electrons give rise to organized living beings?

This distrust of the physical forces, or our disbelief in their ability to give rise to life, is like a survival in us of the Calvinistic creed of our fathers. The world of inert matter is dead in trespasses and sin and must be born again before it can enter the kingdom of the organic. We must supplement the natural forces with the spiritual, or the supernatural, to get life. The common or carnal nature, like the natural man, must be converted, breathed upon by the non-natural or divine, before it can rise to the plane of life - the doctrine of Paul carried into the processes of nature.

The scientific mind sees in nature an infinitely complex mechanism directed to no special human ends, but working towards universal ends. It sees in the human body an infinite number of cell units building up tissues and organs, - muscles, nerves, bones, cartilage, - a living machine of infinite complexity; but what shapes and cooerdinates the parts, how the cells arose, how consciousness arose, how the mind is related to the body, how or why the body acts as a unit - on these questions science can throw no light. With all its mastery of the laws of heredity, of cytology, and of embryology, it cannot tell why a man is a man, and a dog is a dog. No cell-analysis will give the secret; no chemical conjuring with the elements will reveal why in the one case they build up a head of cabbage, and in the other a head of Plato.

It must be admitted that the scientific conception of the universe robs us of something - it is hard to say just what - that we do not willingly part with; yet who can divest himself of this conception? And the scientific conception of the nature of life, hard and unfamiliar as it may seem in its mere terms, is difficult to get away from. Life must arise through the play and transformations of matter and energy that are taking place all around us; though it seems a long and impossible road from mere chemistry to the body and soul of man. But if life, with all that has come out of it, did not come by way of matter and energy, by what way did it come? Must we have recourse to the so-called supernatural? - as Emerson's line puts it, -

"When half-gods go, the gods arrive."

When our traditional conception of matter as essentially vulgar and obstructive and the enemy of the spirit gives place to the new scientific conception of it as at bottom electrical and all-potent, we may find the poet's great line come true, and that for a thing to be natural, is to be divine. For my own part, I do not see how we can get intelligence out of matter unless we postulate intelligence in matter. Any system of philosophy that sees in the organic world only a fortuitous concourse of chemical atoms, repels me, though the contradiction here implied is not easily cleared up. The theory of life as a chemical reaction and nothing more does not interest me, but I am attracted by that conception of life which, while binding it to the material order, sees in the organic more than the physics and chemistry of the inorganic - call it whatever name you will - vitalism, idealism, or dualism.

In our religious moods, we may speak, as Theodore Parker did, of the universe as a "handful of dust which God enchants," or we may speak of it, as Goethe did, as "the living garment of God"; but as men of science we can see it only as a vast complex of forces, out of which man has arisen, and of which he forms a part. We are not to forget that we are a part of it, and that the more we magnify ourselves, the more we magnify it; that its glory is our glory, and our glory its glory, because we are its children. In some way utterly beyond the reach of science to explain, or of philosophy to confirm, we have come out of it, and all we are or can be, is, or has been, potential in it.

IX

The evolution of life is, of course, bound up with the evolution of the world. As the globe has ripened and matured, life has matured; higher and higher forms - forms with larger and larger brains and more and more complex nerve mechanisms - have appeared.

Physicists teach us that the evolution of the primary elements - hydrogen, oxygen, nitrogen, carbon, calcium, and the like - takes place in a solar body as the body cools. As temperature decreases, one after another of the chemical elements makes its appearance, the simpler elements appearing first, and the more complex compounds appearing last, all apparently having their origin in some simple parent element. It appears as if the evolution of life upon the globe had followed the same law and had waited upon the secular cooling of the earth.

Does not a man imply a cooler planet and a greater depth and refinement of soil than a dinosaur? Only after a certain house-cleaning and purification of the elements do higher forms appear; the vast accumulation of Silurian limestone must have hastened the age of fishes. The age of reptiles waited for the clearing of the air of the burden of carbon dioxide. The age of mammals awaited the deepening and the enrichment of the soil and the stability of the earth's crust. Who knows upon what physical conditions of the earth's elements the brain of man was dependent? Its highest development has certainly taken place in a temperate climate. There can be little doubt that beyond a certain point the running-down of the earth-temperature will result in a running-down of life till it finally goes out. Life is confined to a very narrow range of temperature. If we were to translate degrees into miles and represent the temperature of the hottest stars, which is put at 30,000 degrees, by a line 30,000 miles long, then the part of the line marking the limits of life would be approximately three hundred miles.

Life does not appear in a hard, immobile, utterly inert world, but in a world thrilling with energy and activity, a world of ceaseless transformations of energy, of radio-activity, of electromagnetic currents, of perpetual motion in its ultimate particles, a world whose heavens are at times hung with rainbows, curtained with tremulous shifting auroras, and veined and illumined with forked lightnings, a world of rolling rivers and heaving seas, activity, physical and chemical, everywhere. On such a world life appeared, bringing no new element or force, but setting up a new activity in matter, an activity that tends to check and control the natural tendency to the dissipation and degradation of energy. The question is, Did it arise through some transformation of the existing energy, or out of the preexisting conditions, or was it supplementary to them, an addition from some unknown source? Was it a miraculous or a natural event? We shall answer according to our temperaments.

One sees with his mind's eye this stream of energy, which we name the material universe, flowing down the endless cycles of time; at a certain point in its course, a change comes over its surface; what we call life appears, and assumes many forms; at a point farther along in its course, life disappears, and the eternal river flows on regardless, till, at some other point, the same changes take place again. Life is inseparable from this river of energy, but it is not coextensive with it, either in time or in space.

In midsummer what river-men call "the blossoming of the water" takes place in the Hudson River; the water is full of minute vegetable organisms; they are seasonal and temporary; they are born of the midsummer heats. By and by the water is clear again. Life in the universe seems as seasonal and fugitive as this blossoming of the water. More and more does science hold us to the view of the unity of nature - that the universe of life and matter and force is all natural or all supernatural, it matters little which you call it, but it is not both. One need not go away from his own doorstep to find mysteries enough to last him a lifetime, but he will find them in his own body, in the ground upon which he stands, not less than in his mind, and in the invisible forces that play around him. We may marvel how the delicate color and perfume of the flower could come by way of the root and stalk of the plant, or how the crude mussel could give birth to the rainbow-tinted pearl, or how the precious metals and stones arise from the flux of the baser elements, or how the ugly worm wakes up and finds itself a winged creature of the air; yet we do not invoke the supernatural to account for these things.

It is certain that in the human scale of values the spirituality of man far transcends anything in the animal or physical world, but that even that came by the road of evolution, is, indeed, the flowering of ruder and cruder powers and attributes of the life below us, I cannot for a moment doubt. Call it a transmutation or a metamorphosis, if you will; it is still within the domain of the natural. The spiritual always has its root and genesis in the physical. We do not degrade the spiritual in such a conception; we open our eyes to the spirituality of the physical. And this is what science has always been doing and is doing more and more - making us familiar with marvelous and transcendent powers that hedge us about and enter into every act of our lives. The more we know matter, the more we know mind; the more we know nature, the more we know God; the more familiar we are with the earth forces, the more intimate will be our acquaintance with the celestial forces.

X

When we speak of the gulf that separates the living from the non-living, are we not thinking of the higher forms of life only? Are we not thinking of the far cry it is from man to inorganic nature? When we get down to the lowest organism, is the gulf so impressive? Under the scrutiny of biologic science the gulf that separates the animal from the vegetable all but vanishes, and the two seem to run together. The chasm between the lowest vegetable forms and unorganized matter is evidently a slight affair. The state of unorganized protoplasm which Haeckel named the Monera, that precedes the development of that architect of life, the cell, can hardly be more than one remove from inert matter. By insensible molecular changes and transformations of energy, the miracle of living matter takes place. We can conceive of life arising only through these minute avenues, or in the invisible, molecular constitution of matter itself. What part the atoms and electrons, and the energy they bear, play in it we shall never know. Even if we ever succeed in bringing the elements together in our laboratories so that there living matter appears, shall we then know the secret of life?

After we have got the spark of life kindled, how are we going to get all the myriad forms of life that swarm upon the earth? How are we going to get man with physics and chemistry alone? How are we going to get this tremendous drama of evolution out of mere protoplasm from the bottom of the old geologic seas? Of course, only by making protoplasm creative, only by conceiving as potential in it all that we behold coming out of it. We imagine it equal to the task we set before it; the task is accomplished; therefore protoplasm was all-sufficient. I am not postulating any extra-mundane power or influence; I am only stating the difficulties which the idealist experiences when he tries to see life in its nature and origin as the scientific mind sees it. Animal life and vegetable life have a common physical basis in protoplasm, and all their different forms are mere aggregations of cells which are constituted alike and behave alike in each, and yet in the one case they give rise to trees, and in the other they give rise to man. Science is powerless to penetrate this mystery, and philosophy can only give its own elastic interpretation. Why consciousness should be born of cell structure in one form of life and not in another, who shall tell us? Why matter in the brain should think, and in the cabbage only grow, is a question.

The naturalist has not the slightest doubt that the mind of man was evolved from some order of animals below him that had less mind, and that the mind of this order was evolved from that of a still lower order, and so on down the scale till we reach a point where the animal and vegetable meet and blend, and the vegetable mind, if we may call it such, passed into the animal, and still downward till the vegetable is evolved from the mineral. If to believe this is to be a monist, then science is monistic; it accepts the transformation or metamorphosis of the lower into the higher from the bottom of creation to the top, and without any break of the causal sequence. There has been no miracle, except in the sense that all life is a miracle. Of how the organic rose out of the inorganic, we can form no mental image; the intellect cannot bridge the chasm; but that such is the fact, there can be no doubt. There is no solution except that life is latent or potential in matter, but these again are only words that cover a mystery.

I do not see why there may not be some force latent in matter that we may call the vital force, physical force transformed and heightened, as justifiably as we can postulate a chemical force latent in matter. The chemical force underlies and is the basis of the vital force. There is no life without chemism, but there is chemism without life.

We have to have a name for the action and reaction of the primary elements upon one another and we call it chemical affinity; we have to have a name for their behavior in building up organic bodies, and we call it vitality or vitalism.

The rigidly scientific man sees no need of the conception of a new form or kind of force; the physico-chemical forces as we see them in action all about us are adequate to do the work, so that it seems like a dispute about names. But my mind has to form a new conception of these forces to bridge the chasm between the organic and the inorganic; not a quantitative but a qualitative change is demanded, like the change in the animal mind to make it the human mind, an unfolding into a higher plane.

Whether the evolution of the human mind from the animal was by insensible gradations, or by a few sudden leaps, who knows? The animal brain began to increase in size in Tertiary times, and seems to have done so suddenly, but the geologic ages were so long that a change in one hundred thousand years would seem sudden. "The brains of some species increase one hundred per cent." The mammal brain greatly outstripped the reptile brain. Was Nature getting ready for man?

The air begins at once to act chemically upon the blood in the lungs of the newly born, and the gastric juices to act chemically upon the food as soon as there is any in the stomach of the newly born, and breathing and swallowing are both mechanical acts; but what is it that breathes and swallows, and profits by it? a machine?

Maybe the development of life, and its upward tendency toward higher and higher forms, is in some way the result of the ripening of the earth, its long steeping in the sea of sidereal influences. The earth is not alone, it is not like a single apple on a tree; there are many apples on the tree, and there are many trees in the orchard.

Choose from Thousands of 1stWorldLibrary Classics By

A. M. Barnard
Ada Leverson
Adolphus William Ward
Aesop
Agatha Christie
Alexander Aaronsohn
Alexander Kielland
Alexandre Dumas
Alfred Gatty
Alfred Ollivant
Alice Duer Miller
Alice Turner Curtis
Alice Dunbar
Allen Chapman
Ambrose Bierce
Amelia E. Barr
Amory H. Bradford
Andrew Lang
Andrew McFarland Davis
Andy Adams
Anna Alice Chapin
Anna Sewell
Annie Besant
Annie Hamilton Donnell
Annie Payson Call
Annie Roe Carr
Annonaymous
Anton Chekhov
Arnold Bennett
Arthur Conan Doyle
Arthur M. Winfield
Arthur Ransome
Arthur Schnitzler
Atticus
B.H. Baden-Powell
B. M. Bower
B. C. Chatterjee
Baroness Emmuska Orczy
Baroness Orczy
Basil King
Bayard Taylor
Ben Macomber
Bertha Muzzy Bower
Bjornstjerne Bjornson
Booth Tarkington
Boyd Cable
Bram Stoker
C. Collodi
C. E. Orr

C. M. Ingleby
Carolyn Wells
Catherine Parr Traill
Charles A. Eastman
Charles Amory Beach
Charles Dickens
Charles Dudley Warner
Charles Farrar Browne
Charles Ives
Charles Kingsley
Charles Klein
Charles Hanson Towne
Charles Lathrop Pack
Charles Romyn Dake
Charles Whibley
Charles Willing Beale
Charlotte M. Braeme
Charlotte M. Yonge
Charlotte Perkins Stetson
Clair W. Hayes
Clarence Day Jr.
Clarence E. Mulford
Clemence Housman
Confucius
Coningsby Dawson
Cornelis DeWitt Wilcox
Cyril Burleigh
D. H. Lawrence
Daniel Defoe
David Garnett
Dinah Craik
Don Carlos Janes
Donald Keyhoe
Dorothy Kilner
Dougan Clark
Douglas Fairbanks
E. Nesbit
E.P.Roe
E. Phillips Oppenheim
Earl Barnes
Edgar Rice Burroughs
Edith Van Dyne
Edith Wharton
Edward Everett Hale
Edward J. O'Biren
Edward S. Ellis
Edwin L. Arnold
Eleanor Atkins
Eliot Gregory

Elizabeth Gaskell
Elizabeth McCracken
Elizabeth Von Arnim
Ellem Key
Emerson Hough
Emilie F. Carlen
Emily Dickinson
Enid Bagnold
Enilor Macartney Lane
Erasmus W. Jones
Ernie Howard Pie
Ethel May Dell
Ethel Turner
Ethel Watts Mumford
Eugenie Foa
Eugene Wood
Eustace Hale Ball
Evelyn Everett-green
Everard Cotes
F. H. Cheley
F. J. Cross
F. Marion Crawford
Federick Austin Ogg
Ferdinand Ossendowski
Francis Bacon
Francis Darwin
Frances Hodgson Burnett
Frances Parkinson Keyes
Frank Gee Patchin
Frank Harris
Frank Jewett Mather
Frank L. Packard
Frank V. Webster
Frederic Stewart Isham
Frederick Trevor Hill
Frederick Winslow Taylor
Friedrich Kerst
Friedrich Nietzsche
Fyodor Dostoyevsky
G.A. Henty
G.K. Chesterton
Gabrielle E. Jackson
Garrett P. Serviss
Gaston Leroux
George A. Warren
George Ade
Geroge Bernard Shaw
George Durston
George Ebers

George Eliot
George Gissing
George MacDonald
George Meredith
George Orwell
George Sylvester Viereck
George Tucker
George W. Cable
George Wharton James
Gertrude Atherton
Gordon Casserly
Grace E. King
Grace Gallatin
Grace Greenwood
Grant Allen
Guillermo A. Sherwell
Gulielma Zollinger
Gustav Flaubert
H. A. Cody
H. B. Irving
H.C. Bailey
H. G. Wells
H. H. Munro
H. Irving Hancock
H. Rider Haggard
H. W. C. Davis
Haldeman Julius
Hall Caine
Hamilton Wright Mabie
Hans Christian Andersen
Harold Avery
Harold McGrath
Harriet Beecher Stowe
Harry Castlemon
Harry Coghill
Harry Houidini
Hayden Carruth
Helent Hunt Jackson
Helen Nicolay
Hendrik Conscience
Hendy David Thoreau
Henri Barbusse
Henrik Ibsen
Henry Adams
Henry Ford
Henry Frost
Henry James
Henry Jones Ford
Henry Seton Merriman
Henry W Longfellow
Herbert A. Giles

Herbert Carter
Herbert N. Casson
Herman Hesse
Hildegard G. Frey
Homer
Honore De Balzac
Horace B. Day
Horace Walpole
Horatio Alger Jr.
Howard Pyle
Howard R. Garis
Hugh Lofting
Hugh Walpole
Humphry Ward
Ian Maclaren
Inez Haynes Gillmore
Irving Bacheller
Isabel Hornibrook
Israel Abrahams
Ivan Turgenev
J.G.Austin
J. Henri Fabre
J. M. Barrie
J. Macdonald Oxley
J. S. Fletcher
J. S. Knowles
J. Storer Clouston
Jack London
Jacob Abbott
James Allen
James Andrews
James Baldwin
James Branch Cabell
James DeMille
James Joyce
James Lane Allen
James Lane Allen
James Oliver Curwood
James Oppenheim
James Otis
James R. Driscoll
Jane Austen
Jane L. Stewart
Janet Aldridge
Jens Peter Jacobsen
Jerome K. Jerome
John Burroughs
John Cournos
John F. Kennedy
John Gay
John Glasworthy

John Habberton
John Joy Bell
John Kendrick Bangs
John Milton
John Philip Sousa
Jonas Lauritz Idemil Lie
Jonathan Swift
Joseph A. Altsheler
Joseph Carey
Joseph Conrad
Joseph E. Badger Jr
Joseph Hergesheimer
Joseph Jacobs
Jules Vernes
Julian Hawthrone
Julie A Lippmann
Justin Huntly McCarthy
Kakuzo Okakura
Kenneth Grahame
Kenneth McGaffey
Kate Langley Bosher
Kate Langley Bosher
Katherine Cecil Thurston
Katherine Stokes
L. A. Abbot
L. T. Meade
L. Frank Baum
Latta Griswold
Laura Dent Crane
Laura Lee Hope
Laurence Housman
Lawrence Beasley
Leo Tolstoy
Leonid Andreyev
Lewis Carroll
Lewis Sperry Chafer
Lilian Bell
Lloyd Osbourne
Louis Hughes
Louis Tracy
Louisa May Alcott
Lucy Fitch Perkins
Lucy Maud Montgomery
Luther Benson
Lydia Miller Middleton
Lyndon Orr
M. Corvus
M. H. Adams
Margaret E. Sangster
Margret Howth
Margaret Vandercook

Margret Penrose
Maria Edgeworth
Maria Thompson Daviess
Mariano Azuela
Marion Polk Angellotti
Mark Overton
Mark Twain
Mary Austin
Mary Catherine Crowley
Mary Cole
Mary Hastings Bradley
Mary Roberts Rinehart
Mary Rowlandson
M. Wollstonecraft Shelley
Maud Lindsay
Max Beerbohm
Myra Kelly
Nathaniel Hawthrone
Nicolo Machiavelli
O. F. Walton
Oscar Wilde
Owen Johnson
P.G. Wodehouse
Paul and Mabel Thorne
Paul G. Tomlinson
Paul Severing
Percy Brebner
Peter B. Kyne
Plato
R. Derby Holmes
R. L. Stevenson
R. S. Ball
Rabindranath Tagore
Rahul Alvares
Ralph Bonehill
Ralph Henry Barbour
Ralph Victor
Ralph Waldo Emmerson
Rene Descartes
Rex Beach

Rex E. Beach
Richard Harding Davis
Richard Jefferies
Richard Le Gallienne
Robert Barr
Robert Frost
Robert Gordon Anderson
Robert L. Drake
Robert Lansing
Robert Lynd
Robert Michael Ballantyne
Robert W. Chambers
Rosa Nouchette Carey
Rudyard Kipling
Samuel B. Allison
Samuel Hopkins Adams
Sarah Bernhardt
Sarah C. Hallowell
Selma Lagerlof
Sherwood Anderson
Sigmund Freud
Standish O'Grady
Stanley Weyman
Stella Benson
Stella M. Francis
Stephen Crane
Stewart Edward White
Stijn Streuvels
Swami Abhedananda
Swami Parmananda
T. S. Ackland
T. S. Arthur
The Princess Der Ling
Thomas A. Janvier
Thomas A Kempis
Thomas Anderton
Thomas Bailey Aldrich
Thomas Bulfinch
Thomas De Quincey
Thomas Dixon

Thomas H. Huxley
Thomas Hardy
Thomas More
Thornton W. Burgess
U. S. Grant
Valentine Williams
Various Authors
Vaughan Kester
Victor Appleton
Victoria Cross
Virginia Woolf
Wadsworth Camp
Walter Camp
Walter Scott
Washington Irving
Wilbur Lawton
Wilkie Collins
Willa Cather
Willard F. Baker
William Dean Howells
William le Queux
W. Makepeace Thackeray
William W. Walter
William Shakespeare
Winston Churchill
Yei Theodora Ozaki
Yogi Ramacharaka
Young E. Allison
Zane Grey

www.ingramcontent.com/pod-product-compliance
Lightning Source LLC
Chambersburg PA
CBHW020500100426
42813CB00030B/3059/J